The World Is Gone

Forerunners: Ideas First

Short books of thought-in-process scholarship, where intense analysis, questioning, and speculation take the lead

FROM THE UNIVERSITY OF MINNESOTA PRESS

(Continued on page 89)

The World Is Gone
Philosophy in Light of the Pandemic

Gregg Lambert

University of Minnesota Press

MINNEAPOLIS
LONDON

ISBN 978-1-5179-1338-0 (PB)
ISBN 978-1-4529-6718-9 (Ebook)
ISBN 978-1-4529-6764-6 (Manifold)

Published by the University of Minnesota Press, 2021
111 Third Avenue South, Suite 290
Minneapolis, MN 55401-2520
http://www.upress.umn.edu

◢ Available as a Manifold edition at manifold.umn.edu

The University of Minnesota is an equal-opportunity educator
and employer.

This book is dedicated to
"everybody" (tout le monde).

Contents

Contents

Preface: To My Fellow Castaways

IN THE EARLY SUMMER OF 2020, I decided to return to Heidegger's concept of "Being in the World" *(In-der-Welt-sein),* believing it now needed to be fundamentally revised *in (the) light of the pandemic.* At this point, it was apparent to everybody that "the world was gone," and I heard this statement from many others over the previous two months, beginning in early spring. Of course, there was also an equal number of deniers in those early days as well, until gradually the reality of the worsening situation was undeniable for most, even though this stubborn realization was still couched in rationalization and qualifications concerning the novelty of the virus, as if what we were experiencing was just a more severe strain of the common flu and nothing that would warrant the appellations of "pandemic" or "plague."

Regardless of this debate over the proper nomenclature, as of this date in late June, well over 200,000 Americans have died from the Covid virus, and more than 1.2 million globally. Certainly, for the sake of the dead and departed ones, and for the members of their families and the communities to which they belonged, I think we should sympathize with the sentiment that "the world is gone," even though no one outside this closed circle of mourning would be capable of understanding the existential meaning of this particular statement that can belong only to the community of the dead. By paraphrasing these statements with the simple phrase "the world is gone," therefore, I am speaking for "everybody" (or as the French have the habit of saying, "tout le monde"); although, I realize that I am not speaking for "everyone." Regardless, whomever I am speaking *for* or *to,* myself included, it seems we must come to terms with the following facts: The first fact is that the world is now gone, referring to the world that existed before the pandemic, at least from the point of view of the present. The second fact we must contend with is that the world to come is largely unknown, and that it is possible that the previous world will not return, referring to the world as it was before, what is now referred to as "the past world," "the world prior to the pandemic . . . ," and by some as "the lost world."

"The world is gone" is originally from the poetic statement that appears in the final line of a poem written by the Jewish poet Paul Celan that reads: "The world is gone. I must carry you" *(Die Welt ist fort. Ich muß dich tragen).* The meaning of this phrase has remained somewhat of a mystery, despite the history of voluminous criticism, especially given that many of Celan's readers—even the most astute—have already assumed they know specifically to whom *(dich)* this statement is addressed. It is often cited alone, outside the context of the poem itself, the specific biography of the poet, or the body of Celan's work during the period it was written. Instead, it has become a topic in a rhetorical sense, and thus has assumed a shallow and false profundity in many of the critical and philosophical discourses that have employed it exclusively to talk about the poetry of the Holocaust. As a result, the poetic statement itself has fallen to the level of a platitude. As one consequence, it follows that the statement might not be relevant to our discussion of the nothingness of *this* world, or to address the most contemporaneous community of the dead. Therefore, if it is to become the object of the following meditations, *in (the) light of the current pandemic,* all its earlier meanings must first be subtracted or at least bracketed according to the phenomenological method, perhaps even crossing out or crossing through *(durchkreuzen),* in the manner of the later Heidegger, which I will also employ here to make this illegibility more visible to the reader: ~~Die Welt ist fort~~.

As to the second phrase of the poetic statement, one can only add to the endless speculation on the identity of you *(dich)*. The first possibility is that the you represents Celan's mother, who appears in many of the earliest poems from *Mohn und Gedächtnis* (1952) as the "one whose hair the sky wore that day," in the figure of "your ashen hair Shulamite." Another possible interpretation is that the addressee here is Heidegger and is intended as a refutation of the phrase "the world worlds" *(die Weltwelten)*. This statement becomes the explicit object of Heidegger's later claims concerning the "saving power" of poetry in the writings of the postwar period such as "The Question concerning Technology," where the figure of Hölderlin is invoked, as if in a seance, in the famous line from the *Patmos*: "But where danger is, grows / The saving power also." Of course, some would find this second interpretation grotesque when measured against the tragedy of the first. However, in a poem that is collected in *Lichtzwang (Lightforce)*, published three years after *Atemwende (Breathturn)*, where we find the first statement, the philosopher is directly addressed as "you, with yourself" *(du / mit der dich)* and described as an "island-channel . . . fogged in by hope" *(Inselflur du . . . übernebelnden Hoffnung)*.

In the second seminar of *The Beast and the Sovereign,* delivered in the prepandemic era, Derrida also conjoins Celan and Heidegger in a mirror-game between the *fort* of the poetic statement *Die Welt ist fort* and the *Da* of *Dasein*, the entity that is always found *In-der-Welt-sein*. Derrida gives this poetic statement its most direct interpretation (in the exergue saying "there is no world, there are only islands"). Nevertheless, I will continue to make the argument that I have already introduced, that this statement does not bear the same existential meaning that it might have today, even though it expresses the same sense. This is not to say that Derrida was merely speaking metaphorically (which of course he could almost never be accused of doing), but only that it would be impossible for him to imagine in 2002 that the statement would actually become true less than twenty years later, and in ways that he could never imagine—that is, that "there is no world," that in place of the former world there is an archipelago composed of 7.8 billion tiny islands.

According to the strictest understanding of the logic of world that is developed earlier in *Sein und Zeit,* if we could imagine a situation in which the world was absolutely *fort,* then by definition there would be no entity that could in any way be called "Dasein"—*if only because there is no there (da) there, just as there could neither be "I" nor "you," that is to say, no possibility of language.* This raises the question of whether and in what way the I and you in the poem can even exist, if only because the minute that there is language there must also be the possibility of the I, and the second there is an I there must also be the possibility of a you (even if the being that is designated by the you is absent, lost, far away, or dead). In the case of Celan's later poems, we must now acknowledge the impossibility of a world that is peopled by the German language, which has been completely silenced by the poet; thus, the entities who are encountered in the poems as I and you can exist only in the language of the poem. In fact, I would even argue that the translation of Celan's later poetry into another language is impossible in principle, despite the mere linguistic possibility, which is why I will not refer to any English versions of the poems, which in my view are only various misreadings all based on the mistaken assumption that they are translated from the German language. It is this new situation of "worldlessness" of the language of Celan's poetry that we might now understand the first phrase of the poetic statement, and especially in the case of the late poems, beginning with "Atemwende" (1967), which start to resemble an archipelago of tiny islands, or a constellation of stars on an infinite ocean of space (in some ways recalling Pascal's infinite void).

Nevertheless, I will argue that the being who speaks from this new situation of "worldlessness" cannot be likened to a purely worldless *(weltlos)* being like the stone in Heidegger's 1929 lecture, which appears next to the animal as "poor in world" *(weltarm),* and the human being as "world-forming" *(weltbilden).* In order to grasp the situation I am describing, therefore, one would need push it to its most extreme limit and imagine that the you being addressed names an entity that in no manner can be encountered *In-der-Welt-sein,* but rather as an entity that can only be encountered in the poem standing opposite to the I. Of course, the situation I am describing does not belong to ordinary language, which must always presuppose a world peopled with others who could at any moment become you, but rather only in the language of the poem, which Celan describes in "The Meridian" as a "language actualized, set free under the sign of radical individuation which, however, remains just as aware of the limits drawn by language as of the possibilities it opens." It is perhaps in this sense, according to a state of worldlessness that Celan's late poems evoke, that we might understand the second phrase, *Ich muß dich tragen,* meaning that either the being or entity that is addressed as you *(dich)* is literally carried *(tragen)* into existence, or whose very existence is preserved, by the I *(Ich)* of the poem. According to Celan's extreme formulation of language in the poem, therefore, the poem holds its own ground, its own time determined as a present that is not in the world but is "already-no-more" *(Schon-nicht-mehr)*; however, in holding its own ground, the poem nevertheless "pulls itself back from an 'already-no-more' into a 'still-here' *[Immernoch].*" In other words, the *Da,* that is, the ground of the poem is the "still here" and, for Celan, "the 'still here' can only mean speaking." As Celan concludes his formulation of the still-here-still-speaking place and time of the poem, this is why "I must carry you" *(ich muß dich tragen),* if only because the poem is "still here" and "still speaking" that the I needs a you in order to speak, to continue speaking, and this you can even be an "altogether other" *(ganz Anderen),* since "for the poem, everything and everybody is a figure of this other toward which it is heading." Therefore, the conversation between an I *(Ich)* and a you *(dich)* that is actualized by the poem, a conversation that can only take place in the language of the poem, *everyone* and *everything* can become you, including those beings that Heidegger already defined as being without world *(weltlos).*

- A xeroxed copy of "The Question concerning Technology" that I had folded and stuck into my copy of *Sein und Zeit* at some point, which I found in the crevice a tree.
- The Klosterman paperback of Heidegger's 1929 seminar *Die Grundbegriffe der Metaphysik* still wrapped in plastic (the least-damaged book in my collection, as if it bears no trace of the catastrophe).
- A hardback copy of Derrida's 2002 seminar on *The Beast and the Sovereign, vol. 2.*
- The three small blue cloth volumes of Suhrkamp's *Paul Celan: Gesammelte Werke* (probably the most prized possession in my entire library).
- A small pocket-book edition of Emmanuel Levinas's *De l'Existence à existents.*
- The *Collected Works of St. John of the Cross.*
- Deleuze's *Logique du sens,* which I found days later floating on the other side of the island, which now looks more like a conch or sea anemone.
- Michel Tournier's novel *Vendredi ou les limbes du Pacifique.*
- J. M. Coetzee's *Foe.*
- Albert Camus's *La Peste,* on the cover is a picture of a feral black cat on the streets of Oran, Algeria.
- John Berryman's book of poetry, *The Dream Songs.*
- Finally, a shrink-wrapped copy of Roland Végső's *Worldlessness after Heidegger: Phenomenology, Psychoanalysis, Deconstruction* (Edinburgh, 2020), which is the only "secondary source" I had thought to bring along, since Végső's analysis of the theme "worldlessness" in Heidegger was an inspiration, even before the island became real and no longer merely theoretical.

I will provide a more complete list at the end, including the translated English versions of the above titles that I brought for reference, but these thirteen books make up my entire "Desert Island Library" and will have to suffice in place of a formal bibliography or footnotes in the following reflections. My plan is to meditate on a particular book each day (though the difference between day and night will become a constant theme of my reflections, since I have already lost all track of time): however, this should be sufficient citation for the reader to follow my tracks around the island. As far as any scant references to other texts, they are purely from my own bad or weak memory, so I hope that the reader will excuse any gross inaccuracies and that the editor will not ask me to provide proper citations (which I will refuse owing to the same issue of weak memory). *In any case, I would argue, one cannot be shipwrecked and bring along the entire library!* That would be a pure fiction! Moreover, in adhering strictly to the rustic limitations of my chosen genre, *there was no internet on my island.* In other words, when living on a desert island—that is, if one wants to call this "living"—one is forced to make do with what one already has to hand, that is, to exist "with no provisions but an open face" (Led Zeppelin, "Kashmir").

Fayetteville, New York, June 29, 2020

First Day: The Darkening of the World (Heidegger)

June 30, 2020

> The plane is no longer standing on the runway ready to take off. Instead, it is in the hanger being disassembled for spare parts. Outside there are long rows of aircraft like cattle waiting for the slaughterhouse.

The above description is not from a dream, but something I saw on CNN before I ended up on my island. It is offered here as a counterpoint to the famous example from "The Question Concerning Technology" that establishes the essential nature of modern technology, revealing what Heidegger calls the "standing reserve" (*Bestand*). According to the well-known argument, nature no longer produces naturally out of itself as *phúsis,* but rather is "set upon," "challenged," "ordered" by the technological apparatus; thus, everywhere everything is ordered to stand by, to immediately be on hand, indeed, to stand there so it will be on call "for further orders." For example, "The airplane stands on the taxi-strip . . . for this it must be in its whole structure and every one of its constituent parts itself on call for duty, ready for take-off."

For the airplane to be ready in its "whole structure and all of its constituent parts," it means that the pilots are in the cockpit doing their final checklist, the flight attendants have run through their safety presentation, the customers are in their seats and belted in, but also that the baggage has been loaded, the flight engineers have run the required maintenance, the ticketing agents have counted all the passengers, the tower has been notified, the transportation agencies have everything ready to go on the other end, the hotels have cleaned the rooms and they are ready for occupancy, the corporations have confirmed that the meeting is scheduled at 13:00, the tourist company has already dispatched their guides to the airport to meet the tour group, the ship is waiting at the dock in Amsterdam to take the next cruise up the Rhine, and so on and so forth. In other words, if we would carefully follow every switch and relay, we would gradually see the world appears to be connected everywhere and coordinated at every point as if in a vast symphony from one invisible conductor. Now, if we were to multiply this one example by a factor of 102,000, which was the number of flights per day worldwide on July 30, 2019, we might begin to glimpse an aspect of "the whole structure and all its constituent parts," but this would only reveal a partial representation of the manner in which the "world worlds" (*Die Weltwelten*) under the regime of technological challenging, according to Heidegger's argument.

However, if we attempt to trace out only a few of the constituent parts belonging to the whole structure of technological "enframing" (*Ge-Stell*) just a year later from the counter-example offered above, we would see that the pilots are not in the cockpit and the flight attendants have been laid off, only a few customers are in their seats and most of the plane is empty, the mechanics are in the hangers taking the planes apart rather than getting them ready for takeoff belted in, the ticketing agents have been furloughed, the tower is running on a skeleton staff, the transportation agencies have fired most of the drivers and the hotels are less than 40 percent occupancy, the corporations have canceled their meeting and are doing it via Zoom, the tourist companies are closed for the season, and the ship is rusting below the waterline and has to be dry-docked in Rotterdam, and all the destinations along the Rhine are under quarantine and closed to all tourism.

What the counterexample reveals is a major fault line in

Heidegger's argument concerning the essential power revealed by technology—and by the whole structure of the global economy—as an unlimited and over-powering nature that was projected based on atomic energy in the 1950s, and which had only, as its furthest and most external limit, the end of the world brought about in a nuclear holocaust. Today, it is clear to everybody (tout le monde) that the power of technology and economy has crashed into the limit revealed in the power of another nature, perhaps on a molecular level, which is the overpowering nature of life itself. (Concerning this other domain, to his credit, in the 1929 seminar on the concept of world, Heidegger himself admits that life is "a domain of openness which possesses as wealth [i.e., standing reserve] with which the human world may have nothing to compare"). It is not that the "naturing nature" (*Natura naturans*) that was revealed as the dominant ordering principle of the technological and economic expansion of the postwar boom era, or later, the fundamental mechanism of the era of globalization that followed for the last fifty years, is completely in default. For example, one can still hear the arguments from politicians and technocrats that basically still depict the global economy as a "standing reserve" (*Bestand*), and that "once the pandemic is over," the economy in its "whole structure and in all its constituent parts" that have simply been sitting there idling like the airplane on the taxi strip will suddenly receive its order to take off. Even the rise of the global markets during the pandemic, based on hedging bets on the outcomes, holds to this view of the total economy as a standing reserve. And yet, simply based on our counterexample, this does not seem likely, or at least not all at once, if only because a machine cannot function properly when many of its parts are either missing or lost altogether.

What the outbreak of Covid in the spring of 2020 has revealed is a crack in the world that was revealed by technological enframing. In other words, what initially appeared in the whole structure and between all its constituent parts was a thousand tiny hairline fractures, which have gradually widened to become the size of the Grand Canyon. This is not to say that the world is not still technologically enframed, but only that the frame is shrinking today. Perhaps a better way of describing this is to say that another nature that exceeded the previous frame—a nature that, as of yet, *has no relation to world!*—has intervened to cover the entire canvas with dark splotches, as if the overpowering nature of life itself is in the process of "deconstructing" *(abbauenden)* the world-picture that belonged to the age of technology. Therefore, if we could gather around this picture, we might all agree with some confidence that *that world-view is now gone!* What it depicts is *in the past,* and thus the picture itself can now be placed in a museum along with other antiquities and artifacts that were useful and belonged to past worlds, like sawmills and sailing ships. As in the description of the museum in William Carlos Williams's *Paterson,* moreover, there is no picture of the world outside the museum's architectural frame of glass and flowers. In fact, perhaps as a final refutation of Heidegger's arguments in the 1950 essay, it is more than a little ironic that today *everybody knows that only Science will save us! Not only humans, but also animals and plants, and even the world itself!* Would anyone today take seriously Heidegger's early counterclaim that only poetry will save us? Not likely, and I can only imagine that the bucolic German philosopher would be laughed out of the ICU ward for being even more deranged than Nietzsche's madman.

> At this point in my meditation, I realize that it is growing dark and the bright sky is receding beneath the horizon. To make a fire, I have torn up the pages of my copy of Heidegger's essay that I had taken from my copy of *Sein und Zeit* only this morning to read. As each page is thrown onto the pile of kindling, it catches fire and rises in the air until it turns to ash as I fell asleep.
>
> When I woke up, I saw the ashes of the previous world that still littered the beach down to the surf, leaving long rings of brown and yellow foam, like soap bubbles floating on the jetsam of the tide. Nevertheless, I realized that this does not mean I have awakened to a new world.

Last night I established, based on a simple empirical example of the plane no longer standing on the taxiway, that the world described in Heidegger's postwar essay is no longer the same world that has been "worlding" from the beginning of the pandemic. (Apparently, the world is no longer "all that is the case," according to Wittgenstein's famous proposition in the beginning of the Tractatus.) Nevertheless, I have heard many claims that the previous world still exists, and that it is still a "standing reserve" *(Bestand),* like a machine that is simply left idling, waiting for the order to be given to ramp up again and even to exceed its productive output of energy for making more world. According to this view, we are simply in a period of being in-between two moments that are suspended in duration in a manner that resembles Heidegger's definition of boredom *(Langeweile),* which I will return to later. Nevertheless, these statements also implicitly acknowledge that our current duration is not in-the-world; our current state of being-in between is obviously neither in the prepandemic world from which we just departed, nor in the world that will arrive only when the pandemic is over and full economic productivity can resume, even exceeding its previous output, according to politicians. Of course, such statements can easily be dismissed as signs of wishful thinking, or desperate hope that barely conceals the fear that motivates the strength of conviction behind them.

Of course, I am not saying that a postpandemic world will never arrive, or that the pandemic will never end, but rather that when the day eventually comes and we resume some measure of normal economic activity, we will have already forgotten how the *world worlds.* In other words, following Heidegger's earlier existential analytic of Dasein (which I continue to privilege over the later ontology), our existential knowledge of being-in-the-world *(In-der-Welt-sein)* is primordially formed by familiar everyday experience and habit, not by epistemological reflection or representation, nor by our technological mediations of a common world. Consequently, given the duration of being-in-between two worlds where we now inhabit, and will continue to tarry in for an uncertain and perhaps immeasurable period of time, our existential comportment toward what is being-in-the-world is already undergoing change, along with our sense of what is most familiar and everyday experience. In other words, what was most familiar to us before is now appearing unfamiliar, strange, and uncanny (*unheimlich*); this is because today what is most unfamiliar to everybody (tout le monde) is being-in-the world *as such*.

Recalling Heidegger's earlier analysis of "equipment" (*das Zeug*) in establishing our relation to world, in many ways the plane that is no longer on the runway ready for takeoff can be compared to the broken hammer, which no longer appears "ready-to-hand" or "standing to attention" (*Zuhandenheit*), but instead becomes peculiarly "conspicuous" (*auffällig*), which marks the passage from familiar to the strangely unfamiliar and uncanny. Here, we should also recall that the German sense of *unheimlich* employed by Heidegger (and also by Freud during the same period) designates something that was once familiar or "homely" that suddenly becomes "unfamiliar," but in the existential sense of becoming "an unfamiliar familiar." For example, the ghost of a loved one who appears in my dreams brings with her this sense of being an *unfamiliar familiar,* which also relates the feeling of the uncanny to the normal processes of mourning and melancholia. The face of a loved one who recently died, or who suddenly left home, constantly returns in my thoughts and visions, and her visitation becomes strangely not at home, a ghost of the familiar.

Following the excellent commentary provided by Roland Végsó on the first division of *Sein und Zeit,* if Dasein is always already in relation to world, this world first manifests itself as the referential totality of things "at hand (*Zuhandenheit*).... It belongs to the being of these beings that they refer to other things. . . . Reference here simply means that useful objects that surround us in our everyday circumspect taking care of things point to other objects and, through these relations, also refer to a contextual totality. . . . This totality is what we call world in the phenomenological sense." But what happens when, as in the example of the canceled flight that pointed to the entire structure and all its component parts, many of the "references" *(verweisungen)* are no longer "at hand," having been either negated, lost, destroyed, decommissioned, taken out of the totality, or no longer "referred" *(verweisen)* to "the whole structure in all its constituent parts"? For example, when the pilots are no longer in the cockpit, the transportation vans are no longer waiting at the airport, the ship is no longer moored at the dock, or the plane is no longer on the taxi strip, but in the hangar being stripped for parts? When this event occurs, as has clearly happened, according to Heidegger's original argument, then the different constituent parts that are longer "ready-to-hand" (or, in this case, "ready for takeoff") are suddenly "just present-to-hand and no more" *(nur noch Vorhandenes)*. This event is what Heidegger defines as the "disruption of reference," whereby the totality of references becomes explicit. In other words, it is at this moment that something like the world first appears, but its first appearance is occasioned by something like a state of worldlessness. "The context of useful things is lit up, not as a totality never seen before, but as a totality that has continually been seen beforehand in our circumspection. But with this totality, world makes itself known." However, this totality only makes itself "known" by "bidding farewell" (Heidegger) to the totality to which it once belonged (i.e., the world).

The most crucial passage from the first division of *Sein und Zeit* that describes this situation of worldlessness is the following one:

> That the world does not "consist" of the ready-to-hand shows itself in the fact (among others) that whenever the world is lit up in the modes of concern which we have been Interpreting, the ready-to-hand becomes deprived of its worldhood so that Being-just-present-at-hand comes to the fore. If, in our everyday concern with the 'environment', it is to be possible for equipment ready-to-hand to be encountered in its "Being-in-itself" *[in seinem "An-sich-sein"]*, then those assignments and referential totalities in which our circumspection "is absorbed" cannot become a theme for that circumspection any more than they can for grasping things "thematically" but non-circumspectively. If it is to be possible for the ready-to-hand not to emerge from its inconspicuousness, the world must not announce itself. And it is in this that the Being-in-itself of entities which are ready-to-hand has its phenomenal structure constituted.

At this point, before progressing to the next step on a path that has been trodden on by so many others—and is not at all like the barren and rocky beach that stretches out before me now—I will simply say that the hammer was never the best example that Heidegger could have chosen to represent "equipment" (*das Zeug*). In fact, a much more complicated machine should have been chosen to even begin to make visible the structure of references that constitute a world. Perhaps Heidegger chose the hammer simply because it was nearest to hand, but I suspect it is also because he hated more complex machines like airplanes, nuclear accelerators, and atomic bombs. (I can only imagine that Heidegger wrote *Sein und Zeit,* and certainly the later "Question concerning Technology," with the same knit stocking cap on his head.) It's just that the image of an archaic tool like a hammer, which is too determined to belong to the history of "handicraft," stands in the way of demonstrating the totality of references and assignments that make up the structure of equipment, particularly more technologically advanced equipment. In fact, Heidegger himself states quite categorically that "taken strictly, there 'is' no such thing as *an equipment*" (*Ein Zeug "ist" strenggonommen nie*).

Likewise, I don't think that the technical term "reference" is a good choice for the translation of *Verweisung,* if only because it too quickly resembles the linguistic sign; and in the section that follows the introduction of this term, Heidegger takes great pains to "deconstruct" the signifying character in representing all *verweisungen* that make up the whole structure of what he calls "equipmentality." In first introducing the term, Heidegger writes: "In the 'in order to' as a structure there lies a referral of something to something." The original German text reads: *In der Struktur "Um-zu" liegt eine Verweisung von etwas auf etwas.* The translators admit that there is no clear equivalent for the use of the term *Verweisung,* so they decided to split the difference and translate it both as "reference" and "assignment." (The Stambaugh translation, if I remember correctly, also maintains the word "reference" for *Verweisung.*) Henceforth, I have chosen to sometimes employ the word "referral" in place

of the terms "assignment" and "reference." The specific problem I
have with "reference" as a translation of *Verweisung* is that it is too
closely telescoped on the specific character of linguistic signs, or
signifiers. However, Heidegger immediately clarifies in the beginning of the next section on *Verweisung und Zeichen* by saying that
"although every reference is a relation, not every relation is a reference" (*Jede "Zeigung" ist eine Verweisung, aber nicht jedes verweisen
ist ein Zeigung*). In part, this is because the German word contains
the verb *weisen* as a root, meaning "to point," which Heidegger will
later employ to anchor the phenomenology of signs (*die Zeichen*)
by the manner in which they "show" something by pointing away
from themselves toward something else.

However, the crucial point to be demonstrated—*zeigen* also
means "to demonstrate"—is the phenomenological manner in
which signs themselves disappear in pointing to another being
and causing it to "light up," which is a poetic representation of the
signifying character of the sign. Of course, this same disappearing-
appearing character echoes the function of equipment (*das Zeug*)
that is "ready-to-hand" and not "present-to-hand," and this relationship between these senses is poetically reinforced by the close
alliteration between *das Zeug, zeigen, die Zeichen,* and so on. For
example, Heidegger's first demonstration of the sign is the arrow
on the speedometer of an automobile that points to the speed of the
car but is also connected structurally to the equipmental-context
of vehicles and traffic regulations, in short, to "the whole structure
and all of the constituent parts" of technological transportation. Of
course, the operator of this connection is Dasein, the driver, who
maintains a mobile equilibrium between the sign of the speedometer and the road sign that posts the speed limit; moreover, this
also prepares for the distinction between authentic and inauthentic states of existence that defines a possibility for Dasein, since
when Dasein is driving it must operate like every other Dasein
(*Das Mann*) by obeying the speed limit as well as all the other signs
that determine the whole structure of traffic signals. Dasein only
drives authentically (*eigentlich*) when it is speeding and breaking

the rules; hence, the freedom associated with the joys of speeding and not obeying traffic regulations.

Returning to our reflection, prior to connecting the circumspective manner according to which the world of references is "pre-disclosed" by our careful dealing with things and the character of "signs" (*Zeichen*) that will serve as useful equipment for "lighting up" the structure of this pre-ontological disclosure, Heidegger makes several preliminary assumptions at this step that I will now question *in (the) light of the pandemic*. First, he must assume that the world was already disclosed simply by the fact it is always already "laid open" by our circumspective dealings with things, and because there is something like a world of things that is already accessible to our concern. Thus "any concern is already as it is because of some familiarity with the world." In a certain sense, this is a circular argument, of course. However, it is the second assumption that gives me pause and that I want to place in question. "The world is therefore something 'wherein' Dasein as an entity already was, and if in any way it explicitly comes toward something *[ausdrückenlich Hinkommen immer]*, it can never do anything more than come back to the world [zurückkommen]."

As Derrida also perceived, Heidegger constantly engages in a play of *Fort-Da* between Dasein and the world. He ties a rope that binds the *Da* of Dasein on one end, and on the other to the "wherein" of the world (here, one might imagine those wooden paddles with a rubber ball tied by an elastic band). This *Fort-Da* structure seems to presuppose something permanent and intractable in the relation between the *Da* of Dasein and the *Fort* of the world, so that if Dasein explicitly loses itself in something. That is, if Dasein explicitly becomes *Fort-Sein*—as, for example, Heidegger says immediately following this passage, when Dasein becomes fascinated—it has no other choice than to come right back to the world wherein it already *was*. In other words, Heidegger seems to erect a guardrail to protect both Dasein and the world against certain ecstatic states if only to guarantee that in by passing through the unfamiliar and uncanny the world will not be gone forever. Dasein can temporarily go away

(*Fort*) only to find itself right back in the world where it started. The underlying assumption operating behind the entire analysis from this point onward in the analysis is that Dasein cannot lose the world completely, or rather, it can lose itself only to find itself again *In-der-Welt-sein*.

However, let's now return to the current situation in which "the world is gone" and Dasein no longer finds itself to be *in the world that was* (if this is indeed possible, which is a question I will leave open for now). How then can Dasein find its way back to the world when it explicitly moves toward something in some way that is now unfamiliar? For example, in the statement, "I woke up this morning and the world had changed!"—an experience, by the way, that recently occurred to me on the morning after the presidential election—what does this statement mean and what world is being referred to here? The exclamation refers to a disruption or break that suddenly comes to the foreground and points to the "fact" (still only a feeling, not yet a conviction) that the arrangement of the totality of references have undergone a shift to such a degree that the whole structure has changed in all its constituent parts, but this change only appears in the unfamiliar, uncanny, as a darkness that suddenly engulfs the invisible world wherein Dasein was, and still must come back to. It is at this point that we might interpret that statement "the world is gone" in the following manner: the statement refers to the familiar and invisible world that disappears and is gone; the world that appears is strange, unfamiliar, and filled with shadows of former things and others engulfed by darkness. And yet we also suddenly discover that *darkness is a kind of light too!* Darkness "lights up" (*aufleuchten*) the world that appears in place of the invisible and familiar world wherein Dasein was. Darkness is a half-light of shadowy adumbration that drinks up the distance between my island and all the other islands. According to Heidegger's ontological claim, moreover, it is only by the light of darkness that the world can appear as a "phenomenon"; that is to say, it is by *the light of darkness* (in all manners that I will attempt to describe in the next meditation) that the world as a phenomenon can be modified and undergo change in such a way that statements such as "the world is gone" or that it is *not yet* or *no longer* may now be given a positive phenomenological sense, but only in terms of what the world is *not*.

As I meditated on this last insight late into the night, the sky had already gone black at the edges, and storm clouds moved across the horizon to block the moon. In my "retreat" (a word that Defoe's Robinson also used to refer his simple cave), which in my case is only a large overhanging rock about 100 meters from the beach, I could barely discern the text of *Sein und Zeit* anymore in the firelight, as the last passages were almost unreadable and looked like patches of mud. It was around this time, when the sky was almost pitch black, that I put down the Heidegger and picked up the book of Celan's poetry I brought with me, and suddenly saw what clearly looked like a "navigational beacon" (*Leitstrahl*). At that point, I finally understood the phrase "world is gone, now I must carry you." As if for the very first time, the words that in the daylight looked like small pebbles scattered across an empty white page now appeared like constellations of stars in the night. Having realized that Celan's later poems can only be read in the light of darkness, therefore, before returning to my retreat to go to sleep, I tore a page from the book and held it up against a moonless and dead sky.

Second Day: Existence without Existents (Levinas)

July 2, 2020

> I woke up this morning feeling more hopeful, since in the darkness of night I caught sight of Celan's navigational beacon. Of course, this beacon came from another desert island somewhere far off in the distance, maybe from another world, and I imagine that another castaway could see it as well, raising a faint hope that there are also other castaways sequestered on other desert islands who can now home in on it.

Last night I saw Celan's poems as navigational beacons pointing to constellations of stars in the night sky. This morning I wondered whether if I learned how to chart these constellations from my island that I would find a way to orient myself toward the world that is now gone. So I picked up the book again from my small pile and opened it again to *Lichtzwang* to confirm my vision in the light of day. As expected, I immediately found the names of moons, other orbiting planets (e.g., Saturn), and astrological constellations. For example, Taurus the bull *(Stier)* seemed to be the constellation I saw last night, but there were also astrological signs of other constellations, galaxies, which are described as giant disks filled with starry-eyed premonitions *(Vorgesichten besternt)*. But the poem that finally caught my attention seemed to describe the poems themselves as means of transportation off the island, and this definitely is of interest to me, as it would be for any castaway. The first line reads: "CLEARED also for departure" (*Freigegeben auch dieser / Start*); and the final line of the poem describes the "you" of the poem as actually "lifting off" and "gaining altitude" (*du gewinnst / Höhe*). Therefore, if I began my meditation on day one with the statement "The plane is no longer on the taxi strip ready for takeoff," here we have the image of the poem that is not only ready for departure, but apparently has taken off; moreover, it now carries (*trägt*) "you." I find myself wondering if this is the same "you" (*dich*) that appeared earlier in the phrase, "I must carry you."

Since I can't pursue this question much further today, interrupting my reflections on Heidegger's concept of world, I will only briefly refer to Derrida's quite extensive and somewhat tortuous hermeneutic interpretation of this phrase in several places, particularly in *Rams* (2003), which appears the same year as the second seminar of *The Beast and the Sovereign* (2002–3), where Derrida also clearly acknowledges Aries as a constellation in Celan's horoscope. In both places—rather, in the same place on both occasions—Derrida seems to vacillate between two interpretations of the second-half poetic statement *Ich muß dich tragen*. First, Derrida often refers to the process of incorporating and/or internalizing another person in the processes of mourning or melancholia ("incorporation" in the psychoanalytic understanding encrypting the other's psyche in the unconscious). Second, he interprets the "you" of the statement in the maternal sense of carrying an unborn fetus in the womb. Although he does not ultimately choose between the two alternative readings of the line—in fact, Derrida never chooses anything that is presented in the form of an "either/or," and that is the very essence of a deconstructive style—it is clear that he favors the latter reading since it complements his own concept of "absolute hospitality," a concept that is primarily derived from the ethical philosophy of Emmanuel Levinas. I have always found Derrida's use of the image forced, a bit too obsessively "Derridean," and so I favor my interpretation of the verb "carry" (*tragen*) as etymologically moving something from one place to another; thus, the poem itself is a kind of equipment for transporting or carrying, in the sense of Heidegger's "equipmentality" ("in-order-to"), which is also supported by the reference to the plane "cleared for departure" that appears in the poem I have quoted above. Nevertheless, I realize that my own reading could be accused of being equally forced, especially given my situation as a castaway, which naturally influences my reading the phrase *Ich muß dich tragen.* Perhaps I am hopeful that this line is addressed to *me,* in some way, and that somebody is coming who will carry me away from my own desert island. Since that day has clearly not arrived yet, however, I break off my own hermeneutic digression and return to where I left off last night, reading *Sein und Zeit* before the pages turned to shadow and darkness and I found myself instead gazing at Celan's word-constellations in the night sky.

Returning now to summarize the first day's meditation, I came to the following conclusions concerning the applicability of Celan's poetic statement "the world is gone" to Heidegger's phenomenological concept of world.

- First, the statement refers to the familiar and invisible world that disappears in some way; the world that appears in its place is filled with the shadows of familiar things that have now become strange, uncanny, and "un-homely," as in unfamiliar-familiar.
- Second, from this I concluded that *darkness is a kind of light too!* This is because darkness "lights up" *(aufleuchten)* portions of the world that is now covered in darkness, which obstructs or "stands in front of" the invisible and familiar world wherein Dasein *was.*
- Third, according to Heidegger's ontological claim, it is only in the disturbance of the world composed of things that are already accessible and "ready-to-hand" that the once invisible world first appears as a "phenomenon" (from the Greek *phanein,* meaning "shows itself"), proving that the invisible world can undergo fundamental modification.
- Finally, fourth, from the above claim the poetic statement "The world is gone" may now be given a positive phenomenological meaning in terms of what the world is *not (nicht), not yet,* or *no longer.*

In clarifying the first conclusion, I return to underline the contradictory way appearance-disappearance is being employed here to describe the event that happens when the invisible and familiar world "disappears." That is to say, isn't it contradictory to say that the world that never actually *appeared* beforehand can suddenly *disappear,* or that its disappearance is actually what causes it to first appear? How is it that can we understand, much less perceive, what has disappeared-appeared in this case? This is the question that guides the entire analysis and is repeated at the conclusion of each section in this division; for example, "Why can the worldly character of things be lit up?" However, if one were to track all the uses of the verb "to light up" (*Aufleuchtung*) from the first division of *Zein und Zeit,* one could see all the manners in which Heidegger employs the verbal metaphor of the kind of light that *shows* the world in a certain definite way. To illustrate, I simply picked up my copy and leafed through it randomly, highlighting every instance I come across to confirm this usage:

> Has Dasein itself, in the range of its concernful absorption in equipment ready-to-hand, a possibility of Being in which the worldhood of those entities within-the-world with which it is concerned is, in a certain way, *lit up [aufleuchet]* for it, along with those entities themselves?

> If such possibilities of Being for Dasein can be exhibited within its concernful dealings, then the way lies open for studying the phenomenon, thus *lighting it up [dem aufleuchtenden],* and for attempting to "hold it at bay," as it were, and to interrogate it as to those structures which show themselves therein.

> The context of equipment is *lit up [leuchtet]* not as something never seen before, but as a totality constantly sighted beforehand in circumspection.

> The environment announces itself afresh. What is thus *lit up [leuchtet]* is not itself just one thing ready-to-hand among others . . .

> That the world does not 'consist' of the ready-to-hand shows itself in the fact (among others) that whenever the world is *lit up [leuchtet]*

in the modes of concern which we have been Interpreting, the ready-to-hand becomes deprived of its worldhood so that Being-just-present-at-hand comes to the fore.

But if the world can, in a way, be *lit up [aufleuchtet]* it must assuredly be disclosed *[erschlossen].*

Finally, in a later passage concerning the darkness that anxiety lights up in the world:

Anxiety discloses an insignificance of the world; and this insignificance reveals the nullity of that with which one can concern oneself—or, in other words, the impossibility of projecting oneself upon a potentiality-for-Being which belongs to existence and which is founded primarily upon one's objects of concern. The revealing of this impossibility, however, signifies that one is allowing the possibility of an authentic potentiality-for-Being *to let be lit up [Aufleuchten-lassen].*

Certainly, in all these examples, Heidegger's intention is to argue that the previous way the world was "disclosed" *(erschlossen)* can in no way be determined by the traditional language of "appearances," which can only be applied to things that are first of all "present-to-hand" *(vorhanden)*. In fact, he goes so far as to claim that this mode of being previously disclosed cannot even be inferred from anything that is merely present to consciousness. This sets up his later arguments against Cartesianism and all traditional ontology from Plato onward. In effect, Heidegger reverses the Platonic order between the apparent world and the world of essences here, since it is the most familiar world that is invisible, and the world formerly represented as the predisclosed realm of the Idea is now in a secondary position and may even be inessential to the determination of Being as such. (Of course, this is what Heidegger himself sees as one of his greatest achievements philosophically: "the reversal or overturning of Platonism.")

My second clarification touches on something that may be obvious to the reader already but should be stated again at this point. Heidegger is not concerned with the mode by which all things are present, as in traditional ontology, nor with "any object whatsoever," as in logic, but rather only those things that have already been predetermined or "assigned" (*verweisenen*) to belong to some kind of "equipment" (*Zeug*). Thus when these referrals are broken or disturbed (as in the example of the plane that is no longer ready takeoff), what appears or is suddenly "lit up" (*auffleuchten*) is not "the true world," "the essential world," "the world *as such*," and certainly not the "world in its totality," but rather only the darkening of a region of the familiar and invisible world that has suddenly appeared as an obstruction. However, "the world *as such*," or "the world in its totality," never appears anywhere in the world, even in these special situations, and Heidegger says this quite explicitly and repeatedly. In fact, what appears is only the partial or finite world that has been disclosed by Dasein's own concern that was "*lit up* only with the readiness to hand of that concern," but that is now in a state of being disturbed or disrupted. Of course, here Heidegger is setting the later analysis of "care" (*Sorge*) that will conclude the analysis of the concept of world and will provide the single source of light *and* darkness.

My third clarification concerns precisely what kind of light we are talking about here, which I have poetically phrased as "the light of darkness itself"; although Heidegger himself argues that what shows itself in certain existential moods like anxiety does not necessarily need darkness to show itself: "Anxiety can arise in the most innocuous situations. Nor does it have any need for darkness, in which it is commonly easier for one to feel uncanny. In the dark there is emphatically 'nothing' to see, though the very world itself is still 'there,' and 'there' more obtrusively." And yet in this passage I would strongly disagree with the sentence where Heidegger claims that "in the dark there is 'nothing' to see," which presupposes that "nothing" can appear with or without the need for darkness. Therefore, to demonstrate this point, I will now turn to Levinas, who very early on also rejected this claim concerning the appearance of nothingness as the "authentic potentiality" for Being to be lit up.

But first, before turning to Levinas's description of the night, let's list all the adjectives that Heidegger employs to describe *how* the nothing becomes a phenomenon in these moments, when things suddenly "show themselves" and become in different manners "present-to-hand," but only by being what they were not beforehand. According to Heidegger's description, they appear in the modes of "conspicuousness" *(Auffälligkeit),* "obtrusiveness" *(Aufdringlichkeit),* and "obstinacy" *(Aufsässigkeit).* This is *how* things show themselves and become "present-to-hand," a presence that is described as being obtrusive, obstinate, obsessive, obnoxious, recalcitrant, refractory, damaged, or missing altogether. Some things thrust themselves forward and lunge themselves at us, while others withdraw into the background and seem to disappear from view or vanish in plain sight. Still other things just sit there, becoming obstacles to our concern, so that we suddenly have the urge to simply push them out of the way in order to return to the familiar and invisible world. In all these examples, we should underline the presence of definite *force* that defines the nature of the presence that Heidegger has in mind, which he will later characterize as a conflict or struggle *(Kampf, Walten)* and even as war *(Krieg).* In his writings on Heidegger, including the second seminar on *The Beast and the Sovereign,* Derrida will constantly underline the change in the nature of the force in Heidegger's later writings, beginning as early as 1929 in the lecture "What is Metaphysics?," noting that the word *Walten* never appears once in the pages of *Sein und Zeit,* published just two years earlier. It will turn out that 1929 was also a decisive year for Levinas as well, when he traveled to Freiburg to attend the lectures given by Husserl, and it was also that year that he first attended the seminar given by Husserl's most famous student. (It is significant that, five years later, Levinas will publish his first essay on Heidegger's philosophy, "A Philosophy of Hitlerism.") As I will discuss in the next meditation, it is not certain that Levinas attended the winter semester of Heidegger's 1929–30 lectures on boredom, but Heidegger's turn to "meta-ontology" and the theme of Nothingness is already present in the writings of 1929 onward, and especially in the lecture "What is Metaphysics?," delivered at the Davos workshop in that summer, which Levinas did attend.

Turning to Levinas's description of the same phenomenon from his earliest work, *De l'existence à l'existant* (1947), I will preface my commentary by observing that, in some respect, this work was also composed on a desert island (though not allegorically, as in my case), since it was initially drafted while Levinas was interned in the German Gulag between 1940 and 1945. Nevertheless, as Levinas himself admits in the preface to the first edition published two years after the war: "The stalag is evoked here not as a guarantee of profundity nor as a claim to indulgence, but only as an explanation for the absence of any consideration for those philosophical works published, with so much impact, between 1940 and 1945." In the section called "Existence sans existents" (Existence without existents), Levinas explicitly responds to Heidegger's claims cited above concerning the situation in which "nothing" appears, offering the following rejoinders, which I will scan in a logical form of propositions, definitions, and interpolations:

- First, let us imagine all beings, things and persons, reverting to nothingness.
- But what of nothingness itself? Does it also revert to nothingness?
- Something would happen *[Quelque-chose se passe]*
- Question: What happens?
- Response: *There is [il y a]*, which is not Nothing *[nicht Nichtung]*, and yet not "something" either, but "being in general."
- Answer: Therefore, nothingness does not revert to nothingness, but rather to "being in general."
- Definition: "being in general" is "anonymous, impersonal being."
- Analogy: Night is the experience of "anonymous, impersonal being in general," that is, if the term "experience" wasn't already inapplicable to a situation where is neither object nor subject, this or that, and no discourse [no language, no references], and lastly, "no world" either.

- Nevertheless, there is a presence that remains, which is not the presence of "something."
- Likewise, the disappearance of all things and the "I" leaves what cannot disappear, the fact of being before any election, before one wants to be or not to be, a participation with "no exit."
- Only "being in general" remains, belonging to no one, like a field of forces, a heavy atmosphere, a swarming of points with no central point, or monad.
- *"There is" [il y a].*

Looking at the above description, if the direct confrontation with Heidegger's concept of nothingness is not clear enough, I will place Levinas's characterization of the reversion of nothingness in the night alongside the following two passages in which Heidegger describes the nothingness that appears in anxiety:

> In that in the face of which one has anxiety, the "It is nothing and nowhere" becomes manifest. The obstinacy of the "nothing and nowhere within-the-world" means as a phenomenon that the world as such is that in the face of which one has anxiety. The utter insignificance which makes itself known in the "nothing and nowhere", does not signify that the world is absent, but tells us that entities within-the-world are of so little importance in themselves that on the basis of this insignificance of what is within-the-world, the world in its worldhood is all that still obtrudes itself.
>
> What oppresses us is not this or that, nor is it the summation of everything present-at-hand; it is rather the possibility of the ready-to-hand in general; that is to say, it is the world itself. When anxiety has subsided, then in our everyday way of talking we are accustomed to say that "it was really nothing." And what it was, indeed, does get reached ontically by such a way of talking. Everyday discourse tends towards concerning itself with the ready-to-hand and talking about it. That in the face of which anxiety is anxious is nothing ready-to-hand within-the-world. But this "nothing ready-to-hand," which only our everyday circumspective discourse understands, is not totally nothing. The "nothing" of readiness-to-hand is grounded in the most primordial "something"—in the world.

Now to summarize Levinas's overall objections to Heidegger's earlier ontology of nothingness in *Sein und Zeit,* at this point I will

outline three main objections that could be drawn from his work
during this period.

    FIRST OBJECTION: Levinas critiques Heidegger's emphasis on
the instrumentality of things as the privileged point of access to
the "pre-disclosure of being," especially since this instrumental
attitude can also be used to characterize Dasein's treatment of
others as "things" that can be manipulated or used—including
being used up or destroyed. All things and persons are indiscriminately thrown in together in the world that is "disclosed"
by pure instrumentality, in which others can also be assigned to
basically serve merely as "equipment" *(das Zeug)* for Dasein's
own dealings and projects. In other words, persons are simply
tools. Moreover, just like the things that are no longer "ready-to-
hand," other people can also become "present-to-hand," causing a
disturbance to the basic organization of referrals that Dasein has
carefully set up, that is, the structure and organization of Dasein's
world. At this point, persons can also appear in the modes of "obtrusiveness" *(Aufdringlichkeit),* or "obstinancy" *(Aufsässigkeit).*
They can become obtrusive, obstinate, obsessive, obnoxious,
recalcitrant, and refractory. Relations to others can also suddenly become damaged or broken, no longer serviceable, or lost
altogether as when another departs or suddenly passes away. In
many other circumstances having to do with Dasein's projects
and dealings with the world, other people are simply found to
be "in the way," obstructing Dasein's goals as an entity that is
first and foremost defined by its "mineness" *(Eigentumlichkeit),*
and when this occurs Dasein feels the violent urge just to simply
push all the others out of the way like so much "stuff" *(zeug),*
as Heidegger says.

    SECOND OBJECTION: This follows immediately from the first
objection and is stated explicitly in the conclusion of "Existence
without existents." By calling attention to the extremity of the
existential situation that is posited in the night (and in the "tragic"), "Negation does not end up together with being as a structure and organization of objects," but rather designates a purely
impersonal field without "proprietor or master." I will not take
the time to go back through all of Heidegger's descriptions of
the disruption or break in the whole structure and organization

of references that is manifested by the appearance of the "not" (*nicht*) or "Nothingness" (*Nichtung*); however, we should note that in all the descriptions Dasein itself seems strangely "held back" and "at a distance" from the event, and that the disruption only touches on the eye or the hand. In other words, Dasein may become temporarily "fascinated," afraid or anxious, but its bodily existence never becomes fundamentally disabled, and its ability to "flee" the situation of anxiety by falling into distraction and inauthenticity always seems a possibility and a power it maintains as if "what happens" is always kept at a safe distance as in the manifestation of the sublime. Opposing what he calls an "impassive reflection" on the nothingness revealed in anxiety, in his own phenomenology, Levinas will instead emphasize that those forms of physical embodiment of nothingness that grip consciousness do not let it go as in the experiences of insomnia, bodily pain, and illness. From this we might conclude that Heidegger's experience when writing *Sein und Zeit* could never be compared to that of a real castaway who cannot really choose to flee his own desert island. Thus the feeling of incarceration was never real incarceration, as Levinas experienced in the gulag, nor the anxiety over death ever an encounter with real death that Levinas had to face in the news of the extermination of his family in Lithuania. I imagine that these experiences led him emphasize those extreme "hypostases" from which consciousness could not choose to flee and before which the Ego experienced a passivity that is beyond its own activity and passivity; whereas, for Heidegger, the night of insomnia only temporarily disrupted sleep, and boredom was only an obstacle to falling into a state of distraction. For Levinas, the freedom of falling into inauthentic states of idle talk, distraction, sensual pleasure, curiosity, and so on, were prohibited from the start—in fact, these would be pure luxuries that the Ego, if it had the power, would choose over the horror of pure impersonal Being.

THIRD OBJECTION: Of course, Levinas's most ardent and lifelong contention with Heidegger can be summarized in the following statement that appears at the end of the same section where he also historically opposes the Bergsonian critique of Nothingness to the idea of anxiety in the face of death. However, he writes, "to 'realize' the concept of nothingness is

not to see nothingness, but to die." This last statement expresses perhaps the most severe critique of the philosophy of existence, which Levinas also claims represents "modern philosophy" in its historical opposition to the philosophy of Bergson,
who, we should recall, had been the primary representative of
modern philosophy in France until the turn of the century. The
rejection of Heidegger's philosophy (and certainly Sartre's as
well, even though he could not have read *Being and Nothingness*
in the camp unless one of the other prisoners had managed to
smuggle it in) is based on the claim that death gives us "something to see," even if this something is "nothing." In response,
as Levinas objects, *death gives us nothing to see*, does not "show
itself as a phenomenon," neither does it allow us to take our
distance ultimately; thus, there is no transcendence to be found
in death—*in the face of dying, one simply dies, or rather, perishes!*
Perhaps in reply to Heidegger's infamous claim that man can
truly die, whereas animals can only merely perish, I imagine
Levinas might object: "men can certainly perish too! I have personally heard the news of my family, and of the millions who
are being exterminated just like animals!"

In (the) light of the pandemic, I wonder if we would say the same
concerning the millions who have been stricken down by Covid, and
the millions more that will soon follow? Does their death remain
an "authentic possibility" that also "lights up" the world wherein
our own Dasein anxiously awaits a future, especially since world
only belongs to existing Dasein, according to Heidegger? Or instead, have the dead simply perished in the night, often alone and
without family, their bodies have been carried out under the cover
of darkness to be stacked like cordwood in refrigerator trucks or
like crumps of paper across the floor of air-conditioned football
stadiums filled with a thousand other corpses? In many ways this
recalls the comment by Dr. Rieux, Camus's narrator in *La Peste,*
who was also a "first responder" to the outbreak of the Bubonic
plague in the city of Oran:

Since a dead man has no substance unless one has actually seen him
dead, a hundred million corpses broadcast through history are no

more than a puff of smoke in the imagination. The doctor remem-
bered the plague at Constantinople that, according to Procopius,
caused ten thousand deaths in a single day. Ten thousand dead
made about five times the audience in a biggish cinema. Yes, that
was how it should be done. You should collect the people at the exits of five picture-houses, you should lead them to a city square and
make them die in heaps if you wanted to get a clear notion of what it
means. Then at least you could add some familiar faces to the anonymous mass. But naturally that was impossible to put into practice;
moreover, what man knows ten thousand faces?

I think that the difference between Camus's world and our own is
that today ten thousand deaths in a single day is not so difficult to
imagine. One only needs to wake up each morning and view the
jetsam of bloated corpses that have washed up on the beach having been carried in by the tide during the night. In many ways, the
night in which all things and persons revert to nothingness would
be Levinas's version of the statement "The world is gone," which
for many reasons is perhaps closer to Celan's poetic expression
than to Heidegger's more worldly and theoretical version. Earlier,
I observed that Heidegger ties one end of the concept of Dasein to
the world itself by a rubber band so that Dasein never really loses
itself completely in the night, even in the face of the nothingness
of anxiety or fear of death, since *Dasein can never do nothing more
than return to the world wherein it was.* However, for Levinas, what
is revealed in the night is not the world—in the night "the world is
gone"—but rather the purely impersonal Being from which there
are no exits *(Dans ce sens, l'être n'a pas portes de sorties).*

This raises a question that can only be posed *in (the) light of the
pandemic*: if Heidegger proposes that the world is always virtually
present in the whole structure of things determined as "ready-to-
hand," and this structure is interconnected in all its constituent
parts via "references" and "referrals" *(verweisungen),* then how
many references can be disrupted or broken quantitatively before
the rubber band that ties Dasein to this structure finally snaps and
the world itself suddenly flies off into a dark and infinite space like
a meteor? Perhaps another way of phrasing this question is, *How*

long can Dasein endure in an uncanny and unfamiliar space at the end of its invisible rope before this precarious situation itself becomes familiar and routine—that is, before the statement "The world is gone" simply expresses the normal and habitual state of worldlessness? In other words, how do we know at what point "The world is gone" no longer refers to the past world, but rather to the situation of worldlessness wherein Dasein currently resides? At the same time, it is important to point out that Heidegger was never completely satisfied with the language of "structure" that was employed in *Sein und Zeit* to characterize the concept of world that was "predisclosed" in the entire network of things that were determined in their being as "ready-to-hand," and which only appeared and showed itself as a phenomenon when this structure was disrupted. Consequently, the 1929 seminar can be understood as Heidegger's renewed attempt to fashion a new language for the ontological concept of world, which he does by employing the infamous tripartite formula to investigate the manner by which the "darkening" of the world can again be "lit up" from the perspective of the stone, the animal, and the human. According to the metaphoric formula, what he calls the darkening of the world can be "lit up" in three shades of darkness and light: worldless *(weltlos)*, world-poor *(weltarm)*, and world-forming *(weltbildende)*. Of course, this poetic formula has been misunderstood—even by Derrida himself—as an anthropocentric disparaging of the animal world by calling it "poor."

As Roland Végsó has discovered in his *Worldlessness after Heidegger* (2020), Heidegger himself soon realized that the word "poor" was itself a poor choice of words and would inevitably lead to misunderstandings, and that the first revision of the formula occurs in the collection of notes from 1936 to 1938, where we find the following reflection:

> The darkening and worldlessness. (Earlier as world-poor! Liable to be misunderstood. The stone not even worldless, because even without darkening.) Rigidifying and reversion of life out of the initial opening. Accordingly, also no seclusion, unless the living being is

included—"earth" (stone, plant, animal). Stone and river not without plant, animal. How does the decision regarding "life" stand and fall? Meditation on the "biological."

Végsó also discovers a more complete reconsideration that appears in the recently published *Black Notebooks,* where, unfortunately, Heidegger also manages to dig himself in deeper by making some disparaging remarks concerning the "worldless Jew." Nevertheless, in the journal entry dated 1938–39, Heidegger writes:

> The designation of the stone, animal, and man by means of their relation to the world (see the lecture course of 1929–1930) is to be maintained in the orientation of its question—and yet it is inadequate. The difficulty lies in the definition of the animal as "poor in world," despite the reservations and qualifications made there [i.e., in the lectures] concerning the concept of "poverty." It should not be a matter of being worldless, world-poor, or world-forming. Rather, without *field and world / benumbed by the field* [also soil, territory, environment] *and without world / and shaping the world-disclosing earth /* are the more suitable versions of the question's scope. Therewith the designation of the stone as without field and world, at the same time and even ahead of time, needs its own positive definition. But how is this to be articulated? Surely, in terms of the "earth"—but indeed entirely out of the world.

According to Végsó's astute reading, we discover that two new terms are introduced: field *(feld)* and earth *(Erde).* Moreover, these new terms are now set into relation, but also in opposition, to the world. As Végsó writes, "It is not a surprise then that, beginning in the 1930's [of course, the period is also personally and politically significant, it goes without saying], Heidegger projects an inherent antagonism into the very heart of this world (that, depending on the context, he designates with terms like *Riss, Kampf, Streit,* and *Auseinandersetzung*)." In other words, one could also say that 1930 was the beginning of Heidegger's "down-going" (recalling Zarathustra's journey in the section called "The Convalescent"), a period that begins the philosopher's longest "Error" that also ends in a shipwreck, after which Heidegger finds himself a castaway on his own desert island in the middle of the Black Forest "fogged in by hope," as Celan says. It is also beginning with this period that Heidegger will increasingly define the agonistic conflict with the "earth" *(Erde)* as the self-secluding realm that causes the "darkening of the world," and he begins to recast the entire metaphoric language between light and darkness, or between clearing and concealment, in the mythopoetic terms of *Riss, Kampf, Streit,* and *Auseinandersetzung,* and, finally, war *(Krieg),* in which all the other beings (stone, animal, plant, human, and gods) are fatefully encircled. It is this language that will now color Heidegger's metaphors of the conflict between earth and world that will appear throughout the later essays on the poets, which is recast as the violent conflict between two archaic languages of nature *(phusis)*—poetic *(poesis)* and scientific/technological *(technē).*

On the first day, I already announced my own rejection of the mythopoetic opposition between world and earth that appears to frame Heidegger's later metaphysical language, if only because the publication of the *Black Notebooks* has now made it evident that the earth is the absolute "Ground" upon which the elements of soil *(boden),* field *(feld),* homeland *(Heimut),* and fatherland *(Vaterland)* are founded. Moreover, these terms—I have called them metaphors—are prominent in the writings and lectures from the 1930's, and are only barely concealed underneath other mythopoetic themes that are derived from the German poets, especially Hölderlin and Rilke. (As an aside, this is one source of Celan's *Auseinandersetzung,* with both Heidegger and Rilke in his later poems as well.) Nevertheless, what is crucial to observe is that, immediately after the war, we might discern that the earlier concept of the "disclosure" of the world as the whole structure in the totality of things that are determined as ready-to-hand returns with a vengeance in the description of the essence of technology as "enframing" *(Ge-Stell).* In other words, the entire structure of equipmentality that was relatively determined as the world that was predisclosed through the mode of being-to-hand, even though this structure still remained concealed behind the familiar and visible world, now becomes completely present-to-hand and enframed by technological revealing. Likewise, the characteristic of the uncanny familiar-unfamiliar, which was applied sparingly and only when certain things and referrals were disrupted or broken, is now employed wholesale to describe the presence of "the whole structure" of technology in all of its constituent parts—that is, the essential manner in which it produces and reveals the world.

On the other hand, maybe I was a bit too precipitous on the first night after reflecting on Heidegger's essay that I decided to toss the pages into the fire thinking that this description of the world no longer applied to our own, if only because the plane was no longer on the taxi strip ready for takeoff. However, I recall Heidegger's frequent description of the technologically enframed world as completely "strange" and even as "eerie"—and especially for "us late-born Greeks," if I remember the phrase correctly. (Although both terms are possible translations of *Unheimlich,* there is certainly an affective difference of the intensity in Heidegger's later use of this term.) It is even somewhat ironic that the technological world of *Ge-Stell* that appears foregrounded in the postwar essay now looks almost identical to Levinas's description of the night in which all things and persons revert into nothingness; in fact, the striking resemblance between these two descriptions of Pure Impersonal Being might be called *unheimlich.*

Does this mean, however, that we should now simply abandon Heidegger's prewar concept of the world entirely and accept Levinas's description of the night when "everything reverts to nothingness" as a more accurate description of the same phenomenon? No. First, they do not address the same phenomenon (even though both can be understood to address the different phenomenological determinations of light); and in fact, I will argue that *they are as different from one another as day and night!* For example, Heidegger's phenomenological description of the way that things are suddenly "lit up" by a strange presence—that is, the disruption of the familiar signs and references accompanied by the darkening of entire portions of the world that was once invisible—can indeed only occur in the full light of day in which Nothingness appears. Perhaps this is

why Heidegger negates the night as a cause of this strange and unfamiliar light in which things suddenly become present as uncanny,
because the light of darkness can only show itself as a phenomenon
in the light of day. Thus we can conclude that both the appearance
of world as well as the "there" of *Da*-sein are fundamentally related
to the source of natural light, which is not simply a metaphor, any
more than one could say that for Kant the being of the sensible experience is not fundamentally conditioned by the being of sensation.

On the other hand, in the case of Levinas's phenomenological
description of night, we should recall that there are no metaphors
of natural light. For example, "We could say that night is the very
experience of the *there is,* if the term experience were not completely inapplicable to *a situation which involves the total exclusion
of light.*" Accordingly, there is no "predisclosed" (pre-ontological)
illumination of space for things to either appear or to disappear;
consequently, there is no perspective either (i.e., no possibility of
taking one's distance, no "line of flight"). Instead, in Levinas's description things announce their presence only in murmurs, the
sound of rustling, or the voice of silence in the complete absence
of language and discourse. "Nothing responds to us but this silence;
the voice of this silence is understood and frightens like the silence
of those infinite spaces Pascal speaks of." It is the voice of silence,
behind which there is only a murmuring or rustling of a pure impersonal Being that frightens consciousness and fills it with the feeling
of *horror vacui.* Therefore, it would be completely inappropriate
to say that *in this night nothingness appears,* or that *the not (nicht)
appears as a positive phenomenon,* as in Heidegger's description of
anxiety, because *there is* only a pure void.

Nevertheless, there is still a relation that is posited in the heart of
this darkness that is the existence of consciousness itself (although
without any corresponding "there," and outside the "world of others"), a consciousness that resists being absorbed completely by
pure impersonal Being, even though consciousness cannot choose
to flee from Being entirely. (Thus, for Levinas, being condemned
to an existence with "no exits" forecloses the freedom of suicide,

something that both Camus and Sartre thought was still possible.) Unlike Heidegger's Dasein, moreover, in coming face-to-face with pure impersonal Being, consciousness can only dream of becoming distracted, bored, or falling into an inauthentic state of the "they" *(Das Man)*. Yet this option is also foreclosed by Levinas, since if "there is no longer world" (i.e., "the world is gone"), then there can be no "they." Consciousness is found to be completely alone on its island of night. However, in proposing what he describes as "this extreme situation" of night, where he establishes a confrontation between solitary and personal consciousness and pure impersonal Being, Levinas also discovers the possibility of transcendence as the very condition of personal subjectivity. After all, "To be conscious is to be torn away from the there is, since the existence of consciousness constitutes a subjectivity, a subject of existence that is, to some extent, a master of being, already a name in the anonymity of night."

Concluding today's reflections, therefore, I will return to the earlier question, which was posed in terms of an either/or—that is, either Heidegger or Levinas. Having thought the question through in the light of my own situation, which I am only assuming to resemble the situation faced by everybody (tout le monde) today, I have come to the following conclusion: *if one is forced to choose a philosophy of existence to live on a desert island, then one needs at least two—a philosophy for the day, and a philosophy for the night.* Accordingly, on the next day I will employ both philosophies to describe what I call the two dominant ecstasies that I have experienced both day and night on my desert island: profound boredom, which I will argue belongs only to the day *and to the philosophy of Heidegger,* and insomnia, which belongs only to the night *and to the philosophy of Levinas.*

Third Day: The Two Ecstasies of Extreme Solitude (Heidegger and Levinas)

November 23, 2020

"Ecstasy" is from the original Greek *ékstasis,* the state of "being beside oneself," as in the interruption of a familiar state of Dasein, which Heidegger defines as the "inauthentic" *(das uneigentliche),* since it belongs an anonymous and impersonal "they" *(Das Mann).* Likewise, for Levinas, the primitive state of Being is pure impersonal consciousness. However, in the conclusion of the section we have been reading, rather than locating the disruption (or the "limit-experience") of Being in the "nothingness-interval" that occurs in a rare and exceptional state of anxiety, he asks whether individual consciousness and subjectivity themselves might be located as the cause of this disruption. In other words, "We must ask whether consciousness, with its aptitude for sleep, for suspension, for *epochē,* is not the locus of this nothingness-interval."

For example, each night consciousness reverts to a pure impersonal consciousness by sleeping; insomnia is precisely the interruption of this state of being when consciousness awakens to the night, and suddenly finds that it is outside and beside itself. For Heidegger, the comparative daylight state is boredom, when Dasein suddenly awakens from its normal and inauthentic state of existence; this implies that the normative state of Dasein is work or activity, and boredom is what happens when Dasein awakens to find itself "out of work." In addressing the current situation, *in the daylight of the pandemic,* I can only imagine that everybody (tout le monde) has suddenly awakened to find themselves, at least to some degree, "out of work" and thus prone to long intervals of boredom during the day.

Therefore, even despite Levinas's earlier objections to the instrumentality of Heidegger's language to indiscriminately characterize both useful objects and other persons, we need to recognize that our relations to other people most of the time, particularly those we encounter in the course of our work, are precisely determined in terms of their serviceability for our "dealings" with others in the world, employing Heidegger's term for the actual source of Dasein's "care for others" *(Fürsorge).* In the section on "Being with Others" *(Mitsein),* Heidegger employs a range of definitions of the German usage of the term that span from prenatal care, caring for the elderly and sick, and the administration of social welfare; however, on the other pole, he lists those modes of "deficient care" that range from a simple lack of concern to extreme indifference. In fact, he argues that the greater quantity of our dealings with others in the world, this lack of concern and indifference, is what characterizes "everyday, average Being-with-one-another," even though, contrary to Levinas's reading of these modes of deficient care, this does not mean that persons are merely reduced to things in the same factual social arrangement. "Ontologically," Heidegger argues, "there is an essential distinction between the 'indifferent' way in which Things at random occur together and the way in which entities who are with one another do not 'matter' to one another."

In addition to the extreme polarity of Dasein's "care for others," there is another mode of what could be called "deficient care" that Heidegger does not choose to address in defining the modes of "everyday, average Being-with-one-another," even though it is especially present in all of Dasein's dealings with others in the world of work. For example, in the drive-through at McDonalds, I expect the Dasein on the microphone to be ready-to-hand to take my order, answer promptly and politely, make the correct change, and hand me my "order" immediately upon my arrival at the second window. Likewise, at the restaurant after work, I expect the "waiter" or "server" to be prompt in greeting my small company immediately after we are seated, cheerful and subservient to my demands, patient with my guests' questions about the menu or instructions about special dietary restrictions, and then to take our order when we are ready and deliver it to the kitchen promptly, return within an expected interval with plates in arm and place them correctly in front of each guest, and finally, ask us if we want a second round of drinks, and desert after dinner is finished, and so on. Depending on how "ready-to-hand" they are, we might even consider giving Dasein an extra tip, or toss a few coins on the table before leaving the establishment if we are in Europe. In any case, this kind of instrumentality constitutes the largest part of all our "dealings" with others during the day. In other words, in the world that is "formed" (*gebildet*) by work, Dasein plays an assigned role in the Master-Slave dialectic that has become routinized in capitalist societies, and in such a way that playing the role of a Master is regarded as a well-earned entitlement for completing one's daily assignment as a Slave. For example, even the waiter who clocks out after her shift immediately "orders" a drink from the bartender, and then complains to her colleagues about the bad service. The hedge fund broker who ends a day of successful trading on the floor of the exchange by going to the nightclub on 42nd and paying the prostitute for a blowjob in the rear booth is merely a more "conspicuous" expression of the same Master-Slave relationship that Dasein engages in on a daily basis. Of course, in its inauthentic mode of the "they," Dasein actually never sees this relationship to others as part of a Master-Slave dialectic, since it has grown callous and "indifferent" to its own carelessness in order to shield itself from its own mastery and its own subjugation.

In the case of boredom, which belongs only to the day and to the time of work, the normal assignments of both things and other people can suddenly be interrupted in a manner that is similar to Heidegger's earlier description of equipment that has become broken or found to be no longer ready-to-hand. This can take many forms, three of which Heidegger will take up in the analyzing the existential "attunement" *(Bestimmung)* of the mood of being "bored with" *(sich langweilen mit)* in the 1929 seminar: becoming bored by something *(gelangweiltwerden von etwas)*, bored with others *(gelangweilt von anderen)*, bored with oneself *(sich langweilen)*. *In (the) light of the pandemic,* however, I am particularly concerned with how this analysis must now be revised to address the extreme situation of boredom that one experiences habitually or daily in living on a desert island. In other words, what Heidegger describes as the normal feelings of being suspended, held in limbo, feeling empty and disinterested in doing anything whatsoever—especially in becoming bored with others and with oneself—how do these feelings stand with us in the profound boredom that descends like a morning fog to cover every part of our island during the day, and then threatens to last forever and throw us into an abyss?

Turning to Heidegger's 1929 analysis, first, we should immediately notice that the first two forms of boredom he examines clearly belong to being in the world *(In-der-Welt-sein)*: sitting at some "tasteless and minor" railway station and waiting for the train that will depart in four hours; sitting in some boring cocktail party and gradually becoming bored with others. Of course, neither of these situations can be applied to our experience of boredom these days. First, if we update the "tasteless and minor" railway station to the modern airport, especially when the plane is no longer sitting on the taxiway ready for departure and most of flights are canceled, we are no longer simply talking about a "minor delay." (Even the executive lounge is closed and boarded up with plywood, and most of the bars and restaurants are shuttered and dark, so Dasein can't go to the bar in order to kill some time between flights.) Second, because sitting in a large group after dinner and smoking cigars in order to pass the time with some pleasant and meaningless conversation is these days prohibited according to the social distancing guidelines laid down by the CDC, it is difficult to become "bored with others" these days. In fact, today these social experiences of boredom appear more like luxuries of a now bygone world, and even the dreariest cocktail parties now seem like pleasure boats leaving the harbor at dusk for the next port of call with the band playing the final verse of "Auld Lang Syne."

> We two have paddled in the stream,
>
> from morning sun till dine;
>
> But seas between us broad have roared
>
> since auld lang syne.

To save some time in our analysis, let's just bypass these first two modes of boredom as no longer pertaining to our contemporary extramundane existence, and turn instead to focus exclusively on the third form of "profound boredom" *(die tiefe Langeweile)*. In the case of the third form of "profound boredom," there is something present in Heidegger's analysis that might be useful in approaching the experience of boredom that has become familiar and a daily occurrence today—that is, *in (the) light of the pandemic*. I would hazard that it is an experience that everybody (tout le monde) who lives on a desert island has become familiar with, but this familiarity only intensifies the feelings of "being left empty" and "placed in limbo" that are associated with the common and worldly moods of boredom and being-bored. This intensification of mood occurs when, as Heidegger describes it, "beings have become indifferent *as a whole* and we ourselves as these people are not excepted. We no longer stand as subjects and suchlike opposite these beings and excluded from them but find ourselves in the midst of beings as a whole, i.e., in the whole of this indifference." At the same time, "Beings as a whole do not disappear, but rather show themselves precisely as such in their indifference"—and here we should immediately clarify from the earlier sentence, this would also include the being that "I" am, or Dasein as well. "The *emptiness* accordingly consists in *indifference* enveloping beings *as a whole*," which Heidegger also equates with the fundamental "attunement" of metaphysical thought. Thus we find in this last form of boredom, for which Heidegger employs the simple phrase "it's boring" or "it is boring for one" *(es ist einem langweilig)*, there is no longer a distinction between Dasein and other beings since "the whole of being" is enveloped by all-encompassing *in-difference* between Being and beings.

Is this simply Heidegger's way of approaching the existential sense of the situation where "the world is gone," and in a manner that more closely approximates the sense that Celan and Levinas probably intend? Yes and no. First, in an affirmative sense, we find that there is an uncanny resemblance between Heidegger's description of the day in which "one is bored" *(es ist einem langeweilig)* and all beings and persons are enveloped by a profound indifference, on the one hand, and Levinas's later description of the night of the "there is" *(il y a)* when "all beings, things and persons revert into nothingness," on the other. I will only highlight (i.e., "light up") a few aspects of this resemblance.

First, in both experiences there is an intensive depersonalization and even desubjectification of the subject, or Ego, in the designation of "one is bored," which now designates an impersonal and anonymous being.

> It is boring for one. What is this "it"? The "it" that we mean whenever we say that it is thundering and lightening, that it is raining. It—this is the title for whatever is indeterminate, unfamiliar. Yet we are familiar with this, after all, and familiar with it as belonging to the more profound form of boredom: that which bores. It—one's own self that has been left standing, the self that everyone himself or herself is, and each with this particular history, of this particular standing and age, with this name and vocation and fate; the self, one's own beloved ego of which we say that I myself, you yourself, we ourselves are bored. Yet we are now no longer speaking of ourselves being bored with . . . but are saying: It is boring for one. It—for one—not for me as me, not for you as you, not for us as us, but for one. Name, standing, vocation, role, age and fate as mine and yours disappear.

The above passage can be placed alongside the following sentence by Levinas from the same chapter I have been reading:

There is an impersonal form, like it rains or it is warm. Its anonymity
is essential. The mind does not find itself faced with an apprehended
exterior. The exterior—if one insists on this term—remains uncor-
related with an interior. It is no longer given. It is no longer a world.
What we call the I is itself submerged by the night, invaded, deper-
sonalized, stifled by it.

Second, as Heidegger further clarifies the impersonal subject of the
experience of profound boredom, he asks:

What remains? A universal ego in general? Not by any means. For
this "it is boring for one," this boredom, does not comprise some ab-
straction or generalization in which a universal concept "I in general" would be thought. Rather it is boring. This is what is decisive:
that here we become an undifferentiated no one. The question is:
what is happening here, what is happening in this "it is boring for
one"?

In other words, could this description of the subject as an "undifferentiated no one" come close to approximating Levinas's description
of the anonymous and impersonal being? For example, the following
passage: "The disappearance of all things and of the I leaves what
cannot disappear, the sheer fact of being in which one participates,
whether one wants to or not, without having taken the initiative,
anonymously." In fact, this sentence is identical to Heidegger's
definition of the *one* in the statement "It is boring for one" (*Es ist
einem langweilig*). I could go on listing passages that show this
resemblance between the two descriptions, but this would get us
nowhere since we don't yet know the cause of the resemblance.

In addressing the negative sense, I will still argue that they are
not addressing the same experience, since boredom still belongs to
the day, while the experience of the "there is" (*il y a*) clearly belongs
to night. Here again we might recall the following clarification by
Levinas: "We could say that the night is the very experience of the
'there is,' if the term experience were not inapplicable to a situation
which involves the total exclusion of light." Neither is this difference a simple metaphor, as if one were to say that what Heidegger
describes as profound boredom is just a form of insomnia that oc-

curs in the middle of day. There is a different physics involved in the night that cannot be coordinated in a general form of spatiality. According to Levinas, this is because "the points of nocturnal space do not refer to each other as in illuminated space; there is no perspective, they are not situated." In nocturnal space there is only a swarming of points in a field of forces. In other words, the day of profound boredom is not like the day where "Huffy Henry hid," as in John Berryman's *Dream Songs,* nor is the night of pure insomnia a night in which "all the world was like a woolen lover."

Throughout his presentation of the "attunement" of profound boredom, Heidegger constantly employs the metaphor of "awakening this attunement" as a manner of saying that it is an experience that normally sleeps during the day and must be awakened forcefully. But even this gives us a hint as to the reason why this cannot be the same experience that Levinas defines as the night of the "there is," if only because one never allows insomnia to happen, or welcomes it freely (at least at first). The approach or "invasion" of anonymous and impersonal being in the night of the "there is" is a horror that startles consciousness, from which consciousness wants to flee—that is, if all the exits were not already blocked off. Therefore, the approach of the night in which all beings, things and persons, revert to nothingness cannot be likened to an essential attunement that happens by a kind of "essential insight" *(einen wesenlichen Einblick),* nor the disclosure of a possible freedom that occurs when Dasein is open to it and "lets it happen": "What it gives to be known and properly makes possible as something possible and only this, as something that that can be given to be free; what it gives to be free in its telling announcing—is nothing less than the freedom of Dasein as such. For this freedom of Dasein only is in Dasein's freeing itself."

Of course, I could go on all day—and all night—comparing these two very different experiences of impersonal and anonymous being, experiences that I continue to argue are as different as night and day, that is, if "being in general" was not already disqualified as a possible experience, given that there is no Subject present in the night—*not even "one"!* Therefore, in naming the difference between the two, I will simply say that they are completely different existential "attunements"—in short, completely different moods. In the case of the existential attunement of profound boredom, the overall and all-encompassing mood is "indifference" *(Gleichgültigkeit)* that covers the whole of Being; however, in the attunement that belongs to the "there is," the dominate mood is one of "horror." Thus, "the rustling of the *there is . . . is* horror." As we already know from *Sein und Zeit,* moods are nothing *subjective*; a subject does not choose to have a mood. Instead, a mood is determined by the existential situation: *that of already being delivered over to Being-in-a mood.* For example, I wake up in the morning and I am already in a bad mood. Perhaps it is only the residue of the night that has vanished, but I am already caught up in this mood already. From that moment onward, I know that the whole day is fucked! I might as well go back to bed, or retire to the darkness of my cave and try to go to sleep, saying to myself, "Maybe tomorrow I will be in a better mood." As Heidegger says: "In this 'how one is,', having a mood brings Being to its '*there.*'"

Moreover, if I could speculate as to the concrete existential situation that determines this difference in moods, it would simply come down to this: the mood of indifference occurs in a world where *Da*-sein is still free, but the mood of horror only occurs in the night, where Dasein—if we choose to employ this term—is already found to be confined. To put this more simply, the attunement of profound boredom can only be experienced by a subject who is in the world and for whom freedom remains a possibility; whereas the horror of a night when all things and persons revert to nothingness can only be experienced by a subject who is confined and for whom freedom is illusory, since, according to Levinas, the horror of a night "with no exits" (that is, to a "Being-in" which does not correspond to a "being there") belongs only to "an irremediable existence."

To conclude today's reflections, I began by proposing that Heidegger's earlier concept of world and the fundamental attunement of Dasein to Being-in-the-World *(In-der-Welt-sein)* needed to be revised to address these extreme existential situations . . . *in (the) light of the pandemic.* I will now conclude by saying that I believe I have accomplished at least a partial revision by posing Heidegger's fundamental attunement of profound boredom in confrontation with Levinas' description of the night of pure impersonal Being. Instead, we have discovered that the difference between the two was like night and day, except that the night of the "there is" does not belong to the same day as when "it is boring for *one.*" In other words, each night the world goes away, as if hurled like a meteor into the infinite void that Pascal feared, and consciousness is suddenly awakened to find itself all alone in the night and completely bodiless, cast adrift on that void. However, each day Dasein still awakens to a world in which all persons and things are covered in a great fog, as if to a day in which all the cows are white, and each successive day only feels it is becoming more and more indifferent toward all beings, including itself. At that moment, no longer capable of returning to a world wherein it was, Dasein can only retreat farther into the center of its own island and try to fall back to sleep, dreaming that one day it will learn to live in a world without others.

Fourth Day: A World without Others (Tournier)

December 1, 2020

After the last meditation on the two dominant ecstasies of the pandemic, profound boredom during the day and insomnia during the night, I decided to return to the fable of Robinson Crusoe to reflect on living in "a world without others." Nevertheless, I will not return to Defoe's original prototype of the fable, but instead to Michel Tournier's perverse avatar from the novel *Vendredi, ou les limbes du Pacifique* (1967). Of course, there is a much simpler explanation as to why I choose Tournier's version over Defoe's, since it is the only version of the story of Robinson Crusoe that I brought with me to my own desert island. Therefore, one must make do with whatever one has at hand. This oversight has also proved to be opportune since, in my view, Defoe's Robinson Crusoe never actually experienced his own shipwreck, and never really departed from the world of others, since he brought his culture and religion with him—packed in watertight compartments in the large suitcases he rescued from the Virginia—and so in this regard he was more of a colonizer than a castaway.

To picture the extreme situation of living in a world without others, therefore, demands more than a simple desert island fable, but a more phenomenological investigation of the subject of Robinson himself. As Tournier's version exemplifies, first, to be "alone," there

43

must also be others, or what Deleuze refers to in his commentary on the novel as an a priori Other, or an "Other-Structure," that in many ways resembles Heidegger's description of the world that is populated by others as a complete structure of references and referrals (*verweisungen*) that constitute the very possibility of subjectivity. I can only be alone apart from all the others, or at a remote distance from the world of others; otherwise, solitude would never be experienced as *my own*. However, given the extreme state of solitude that is being suffered by many castaways today, locked into their private apartments or separate rooms, with or without the company of a companion animal or a Friday, I decided to choose Tournier's version of the fable to explore whether, ontologically speaking, it is possible to speak of a world without others, or of an existence without world, and remain "I" or "oneself."

Taking up my claim that the fabula of Robinson Crusoe has changed sense today, if only because, at least to some degree, everybody (tout le monde) is living on a desert island, this is not intended as an empirical description of the many different states of affairs caused by the pandemic, or by the underlying inequalities of global populations. Instead, it is only a statement that one no longer needs a fable to imagine the existential reality of such an "extreme situation" of solitude. Sometimes it is necessary to place an ocean between yourself and the world of others to reflect on your existence, but the idea that one can choose to become a castaway one day is nothing but a fiction. Nevertheless, the fiction of the desert island still serves a useful and dialectical function as a surface of reflection on existence, which cannot be viewed directly—at least, not at first. (It is a bit like what Plato said about the sun, which can only be viewed in the reflection that appears in a puddle of water.) After all, why do we read novels to look at our own existence? To gain the necessary vantage point? To look at ourselves from a second- or third-perspective point of view? In this sense, the fable functions as a navigational beacon homing in on the world that was once populated by others, which is now called "the former world," or the world that is gone.

Once again, this recalls Heidegger's earlier definition of signs—and what are novels but a certain constellation of signs?—as "equipment" for referring or showing something else *(Verweisung)*, and he also pointed to the way the sign's own phenomenological aspect immediately disappears in referring to something in its place. Is this not also to define the function of a novel as a kind of equipment for causing our familiar existence to become visible and, at the same time, strangely unfamiliar *(unheimlich)*—that is, to give it the status of a shadow or a refection? This is the ontological status of all fiction. And yet, according to the term of my claim that the ontological sense of the Robinson fable has changed *in (the) light of the pandemic,* what use will we have for the fable now? This will be the subject of my investigation.

Concerning the fact that the prototypical Crusoe was never really exposed to the extreme situation we are imagining today, this has been noted before by many others. It was first observed by Ian Watt in *The Rise of the Novel,* who perceived in the description of Robinson Crusoe's neat and tidy island, in which everything has a place and there is a place for everything, the perfect representation of the mode of production and the relations between production and consumption that prefigure the emergence modern capitalism, including a certain Protestant temperament of the dry and completely humorless type of liberal individual that Crusoe represented, a real "bore." As Deleuze once commented, if there is an upside to the fact that children are still forced to read the most boring novel in the world, perhaps it can be found in the completely healthy reaction that it might provoke in them to avoid becoming such an individual themselves.

However, it was Virginia Woolf who first perceived in Defoe's own alter-ego the sad domestic economy of a typical English gentleman, whose ideal intimate companion would be a dog curled up at his feet, and a boy, rather than a member of the opposite sex, who would later turn out to be Robinson's "Man Friday" in the *Farther Adventures.* In other words, Woolf immediately discerned that Defoe didn't need to travel at all to find Robinson Crusoe's island,

and that the South Sea adventure was merely a popular fictional vehicle that Defoe had ripped off from the London newspapers of this period to portray the external space of his own desert island subjectivity. As Defoe himself confessed in *Serious Observations,* one does not actually need a desert island, since "I never feel myself more alone than in the center of a populous city like London." Therefore, it is a lasting historical irony that Crusoe's desert island was England itself, which in the end is only an island that is populated by smaller islands.

The South African novelist J. M. Coetzee would later deploy Woolf's insight in his own version, *Foe,* which is the story of a female castaway, Susan Barton, who narrowly escaped the abuse of Brazilian slavers by slipping overboard in the middle of the night and ending up on the island with the actual "Cruso" and, of course, Friday, "a Negro with a head of fuzzy wool, naked except for a pair of drawers." Nevertheless, Coetzee employs the fable as an allegory of a colonial Afrikaans woman writer who travels to London to confront the famous author, Daniel Foe, for plagiarizing her own castaway narrative, and ends up occupying the author's apartments in Kensington while Foe is in prison for unpaid debts, bringing along with her her shadow, the black and mute figure of Friday. When the author finally returns, Barton holds him hostage and forces him to acknowledge the dubious existence of certain letters she wrote to the author recounting her misfortune and her encounter with the real "Cruso," that is, to admit to the fact that this was really *her story,* and it was moreover real and not simply a fable invented by her "Foe" (enemy). As an aside, even though Derrida mentions the novel in his own reading of the Robinson fable in *The Beast and the Sovereign,* he apparently never read more than the title, especially in the claim that there is "no trace of woman" *(pas trace de femme)* on Crusoe's Island—and thus could be accused, along with the author himself, for eliding the existence of *a real female castaway.* Ultimately, Coetzee's version gradually strips away all allegorical representation and destroys the fable itself by revealing the finger of a "darker author" who is writing on the wall of colonial history, the real Friday who will seal the fate of both European castaways, Daniel Foe and Susan Barton.

Turning now to Tournier's version of the fable, the reader might already have guessed that it narrates the experience of another (*autrui*) Robinson, and most importantly for our purposes, describes the possible transformative and even destructive effects of living in a world without others, which is why I have decided to employ its fable either as a word of warning or sign of hope for the reader and fellow castaway. The novel begins, prior to the shipwreck, with the fortune-telling of "Robinson's" fate as told through a reading of tarot cards by Captain Van Deyssel. As the captain says, "My brief lecture is in some sort of a coded message, and the key to the cipher is your future itself." Each card represents a different stage of Robinson's solitude, from the loss of his original identity due to the corrosive effects of his estrangement from the world of others to the eventual recovery of a new subjectivity caused by his union with the quasi-mythical being of Friday.

The first card reveals the Demiurge, the creator of second order; "There is an organizer in you," says the captain, "one who does battle with a world in disorder which he seeks to master by whatever means come to his hand." "'Mars,' said the captain. 'The little Demiurge has achieved a seeming victory over Nature. He has triumphed by the force of his own will and imposed an order which is in his own image." With these words, the captain stops to reflect upon Robinson's own image to imagine what this world might look like:

> Robinson the King . . . you are 22. You have deserted—that is to say, left behind in York—a young wife and two children, to seek your fortune in the new world, like so many of your compatriots. Your close-cropped hair and square, russet beard, clear eyed steady gaze, in which there is a hint of something narrow and rigid, your attire, whose sobriety is near to affectation—all this puts you in the category of those who never had doubts. You are pious, parsimonious, pure.

Through the voice of the captain, Tournier parodies the portrait of Defoe's original prototype as a young colonizer. If there is a domi-

nant psychological trait that appears in the captain's words, it is the
perception of Robinson's anal character, which will play an important part in the re-creation of the new house economy on his island.
"The kingdom over which you will preside will be like one of those
tidy cupboards where the women of our country keep their piles of
immaculate linen scented with lavender." At this point, as the reader
might have expected, the captain prophecies Robinson's "down-
going" (*Untergangen*), which comes from Nietzsche's *Thus Spoke
Zarathustra,* but also echoes the Heideggerian theme of "thrown-
ness" and coming face-to-face with the "nothing" of the world.
However, the true cause of Robinson's descent was already implicit
in the judgment that underlies the captain's sarcasm: Robinson
is inexperienced, a heterosexual white male of twenty-two, even
though Robinson himself is—at the moment of his tarot reading—
completely unconscious of his inexperience and carelessness to-
wards others, such as his wife and children, whom he left behind
to go on his adventure. (In the original novel, Crusoe's father even
forewarns the young adventurer of the catastrophe that will be-
fall him as God's judgment for his desire to escape his "station in
life" and, in the end, would make him "the most Miserable wretch
that ever was born"). Only the immanent shipwreck will reveal to
Robinson the fact of the captain's final judgment: "The truth is you
have everything to learn."

On the island, immediately following the shipwreck, Robinson
begins to learn the reality of his extreme solitude. The first effect
of solitude that Robinson notices is an immediate distortion of the
perceptual field: "optical illusions, mirages, hallucinations, waking dreams, imagined sounds, fantasy and delirium." This also has
immediate effects on Robinson's natural capacity for speech, or
"actualized language." "Language," according to Robinson's log-
book, "in a fundamental manner evokes a peopled world, where
the others like so many lamps casting a glow of light around them
in which everything is, if not known, at least knowable. The lights
have vanished from my consciousness." In fact, by the time that
Friday arrives on the island in Tournier's version, the power of

language—the identity of the subject that it brings with it, along with the community to which this subject belongs—has atrophied to the point where words themselves appear more like dream images. All associations appear false or strangely distorted, and consciousness no longer glows with the illumination of interiors and the contours usually furnished by others.

Only after a brief period on the island, Robinson's own body is no longer defined as a "possession" of Robinson himself, but appears to resemble a "thing" in a neutral and objective relation to other bodies or objects, which are either present or found to be missing from the reality of the island. Robinson's own perception of his own body is reduced to being purely "present at hand" (*vorhanden*) like a common object merely expressing the predicate relationship of "the body of Robinson," but with no more proximity to the subject than statements like "Robinson's pipe," or "Robinson's goat." In other words, the predicate relationship that language usually expresses is now contingent and can undergo further modification as, for example, when a common object (e.g., my comb, my keys) is accidentally lost or destroyed. By the end of this process, Robinson gradually sheds all the attributes of his former identity such as age, gender, race, sexuality, nationality, memory, perception: in short, the subject of "Robinson" is peeled like an onion and vanishes, layer by layer.

As the duration of Robinson's solitude on the island grows longer, Tournier describes a state in which Robinson's consciousness begins to merge with the island itself, a process that is accompanied by Robinson's descent into the inner core of "Speranza" and the discovery of a secret coombe where he curls up and goes to sleep. In a later journal entry, Robinson himself comments on the significance of the last barrier of his subjectivity that has been dismantled by his experience of solitude. It is at this moment that Robinson compares his state to the conscious recognition of his own physical death in the consciousness of others.

> All those who knew me, all without exception, believe me dead. My own belief in my existence is opposed to that of unanimous belief. No

matter what I do, I cannot prevent that picture of Robinson's dead body from existing in all their minds. This alone, although certainly it does not kill me, suffices to remove me to the outermost confines of life, to a place hung between heaven and hell—in a word, to a Limbo.

Here we might understand this comparison as a more accelerated duration of natural death that is usually made visible by a fatal disease, but otherwise operates invisibly and imperceptibly in the individual's body from the moment of birth. In the above quotation, the mechanism that causes this accelerated state of decomposition is the association of Robinson's name with the picture of Robinson's dead body, which initiates a gradual fading of the distinct presence of Robinson to himself "in the minds of these Others." Of course, what this implies is that the only thing that was holding Robinson's former identity together while he was alive was the very same structure of association that originated from the presence of others; therefore, the gradual release of the others' grip on Robinson's presence-to-himself positively frees him from being *Robinson-himself,* who was, in fact, only *Robinson-for-the-others.*

Nevertheless, this positive discovery also constitutes the revelation of the identity of death and sexuality in Robinson's consciousness. On the sea floor surrounding the island (Robinson's body), a small crevice occurs and suddenly widens, where the earth is ripped open. At first a canyon appears from the small crack of Robinson's anus, and tidal waves spill over the entire surface of the island. The first wave would be a shift that occurs in the meaning of Robinson's solitude, which he initially enjoys with his bride "Speranza" (the earth) by crawling into the dark recesses of her body to deposit his seed in the "pink coombe." Nevertheless, the danger lurking in Robinson's sexual union with Speranza is his continued vulnerability to all manners of "wallowing in the mire," which Freud had attributed to the persistence of the "death instinct" *(Todestrieb).* In other words, surviving the disequilibrium caused by the fear of his natural death, Robinson has managed only to construct a state of affairs that is even further from equilibrium. Thus he will only be saved from this second death, an inorganic death much more terrifying than the natural death he has just survived by the intervention of Friday.

Who is Robinson's Friday? In Tournier's version, Friday represents nothing more than the reality principle that threatens to deconstruct the fragile order that Robinson constructs by means of his sexual union with Speranza. Thus, from the very beginning, Friday's very presence on the island seems to disturb the order and tidiness of Robinson, and his actions fundamentally disturb its strictly economic and prescribed order of days and places, as well as the moral codes of propriety and impropriety that were far too rigidly ordered, like the "tidy cupboard of immaculate linen scented with lavender" that was earlier prophesied by the Captain. At the same time, the introduction of Friday's presence already foreshadows a new understanding of desire that is no longer founded by the notions of possession and property that belonged to Robinson's previous economic arrangements of heterosexual desire. As I have already outlined, the first economic determination of the sexual object was destroyed by the corrosive effects of Robinson's solitude caused by his estrangement from the others. The second economic arrangement reproduces itself by transferring Robinson's desire for a lost or missing sexual object onto the body of Speranza herself. Reflecting on a dream in his journal, Robinson eventually concludes that both of these earlier failures were caused by the residual elements of anthropomorphism that still influenced the sexual organization of his substance.

> My love affair with Speranza was still largely human in its nature; I fecundated her soil as though I were lying with a wife. It was Friday who brought about a deeper change. The harsh stab of desire that pierces the loins of the lover has been transformed for me into a soft jubilation which exalts and pervades me from head to foot, so long as the sun-god bathes me from head to foot.

Finally, the above dream-work prefigures a last phase where Robinson's sexuality undergoes another and final metamorpho-

sis, as was foretold in the tarot reading where the combination of
Robinson-Friday prefigures the arrival of a new avatar of Venus
"rising from the waves." It represents the culmination of the series of
metamorphoses that Robinson's "substance" undergoes that lead to
a final teleological accord with a pure and elemental Desire, which
is described as the coupling of Friday and Robinson, who are born
from *"le Grand Luminaire Halluciné,"* the moon goddess who has
swept the stars from the night sky *(désastre)*. At this point, Robinson
is writing in his journal or dream-diary by the light of the moon,
while Friday is curled up like a blossom or an egg at Robinson's feet.
In this state of enraptured vision, Robinson is finally able to sink all
the way to "the hither side of consciousness" and slip his yoke into
the egg of Friday's hallucinatory presence:

> Vague patterns appear and vanish on the white disc, shadowy hands
> reach and clasp, faces smile for an instant, to vanish into mist. The
> spinning gains in speed until it resembles immobility, as though the
> very excess of turbulence had caused the lunar jelly to set. And grad-
> ually the pattern is defined. There are two poles at either end of the
> egg, with a tracing of lines between them. The poles become heads,
> and the arabesque the outline of two conjoined bodies. Two similar
> beings, twins, are in the process of gestation: Gemini are being born
> on the moon.

In the above passage, Tournier reveals the identity of Friday as the
avatar of Robinson's sexual metamorphosis. Friday appears in the
waves in the figure of Venus who "drives Robinson out into the
region of her father Uranus" and returns them to a state of pure
and elemental sexuality, one that neither colonizes the earth nor
requires a detour through the body of woman: *"The truth is that the
height to which we have soared, Friday and I, the difference between
the sexes has been surpassed."* Robinson is now "a Uranian," so that
when a ship finally appears and then departs, it does not return
home with Robinson (who by now has lost all filiation with his
former species), but rather with Friday, who travels back to Europe
in Robinson's place. In Friday's place there suddenly appears a new
castaway, an orphaned child who steals away from the presence of

the sailors in the middle of the night to live with Robinson (a bit like Susan Barton in Coetzee's version). This is the child who Robinson will adopt as his new companion. Since he comes from Estonia and his name, "Jaan Neljapäev," is unpronounceable, Robinson decides to name him "Tuesday," since *Tuesday is the Sunday of children.*

Concluding my brief précis of the fable, if I said earlier on that Tournier's version is a more realistic account of the extreme situation of living on a desert island than Defoe's original narrative, I would now qualify this statement by saying that this only extends to the account of Robinson's initial effects of solitude (which is more or less accurate, speaking from personal experience). However, beginning with the arrival of the child Friday, and all the metamorphoses that Robinson undergoes from that moment onward, the novel is more like science fiction in the fantastical account of the hallucinatory phenomena caused by Robinson's loss of the world of others. As to the real cause of the hallucinations, I can only speculate, but perhaps he ate some wild berries on the island that produced the same psychotropic effects as LSD, including the final vision of Friday as Venus rising from the waves. Nevertheless, what this illustrates is that both the extreme poles of depressive and schizoid mania must also be recognized as possible "existential attunements" (Heidegger), alongside the normal effects of profound boredom and insomnia, for the purposes of our phenomenological investigation of solitude. A second hypothesis would be that everything that transpires following what I will define as Robinson's schizoid and depressive phases takes place deep in the cave where Robinson is dreaming, and thus everything afterward—including the arrival of Friday, and later, the child Tuesday—is part of the long dream that begins when the conscious Robinson falls unconscious.

Regardless, there are only two possible endings to any castaway narrative: rescue or death. Concerning the ending of Tournier's version, therefore, either we must imagine Robinson curled up in the deepest part of his cave dreaming of the events involving metamorphosis with Friday, as well as the ship that eventually lands on the island to take Friday away and deposit "Jaan Neljapäev," who

becomes the new child Tuesday; or, we must imagine Robinson
Crusoe already dead and what we have been reading is the dream-
dairy that was salvaged from the cave. If this were indeed the case,
then Coetzee's ending of the novel *Foe* is perhaps more realistic in
showing the bloated corpses of Susan Barton, the female castaway,
and Daniel Foe, the author, floating in the stateroom of the Virginia.
Circling above them, on the ceiling of their sunken crypt, is the
dark shadow of Friday on a bamboo raft, throwing flowers on their
watery grave. In applying this fable to our contemporary situation,
I wonder if the end of our own fable will be no different.

Fifth Day: The Schizoid and the Depressive (Deleuze)

December 3, 2020

In an early essay that first appeared in 1967 and published as an appendix to *Logique du sens* (1969), "Michel Tournier et le monde sans Autrui," Gilles Deleuze employs Tournier's "philosophical novel" to pose the following question: "Must we conclude that sexuality is the only fantastic principle able to bring about a deviation from the rigorous economic order assigned by the origin?"

This question must be understood in two senses, the first of which requires a radical revision of Heidegger's concept of world as a "whole structure" and the role of others as constituent parts of this structure by incorporating the fundamental component of sexuality in what Deleuze calls the "Other-Structure." Why? Because, in the case of Heidegger's ontology, one can easily apply Derrida's earlier claim that there is "no trace of woman" (*pas trace de femme*)—actually, no trace of any sexuality whatsoever! The second sense of the question, which I will return to at the end, concerns replacing sexual difference at the origin of human subjectivity with what he and Guattari later call "becoming" (as in "becoming-woman," "becoming-animal," "becoming-molecular," etc.)—that is to say, to replace sexual difference as an origin with the deviation from normative sexuality as a "final end," and so as an analogy to a psychoanalytic understanding of the goal of perversion. Corresponding to both senses of the above question, Deleuze employs Tournier's version of Robinson as an "instrument of research" to investigate the effects of the absence of the Other-Structure in the extremely artificial situation of the fable of another Robinson. As Deleuze writes, "Philosophical reflection can benefit from what the novel shows with so much force and life."

First, what Tournier's novel reveals is the crucial role that the presence of the Other-Structure plays in the entire "organization" of the world from its margin or background, the transitions from one field of perception to the next. In short, the presence of Others already attests to a structural organization of the world in both its center and in its margins, but also operates the possible transitions from the unseen depths of the subject's own body to the visible surfaces of objects. Drawing in part on Sartre's phenomenological analysis of the Other in *Being and Nothingness,* Deleuze describes the normal functioning of the perceptual field that is conditioned by the presence of others as follows:

> The part of the object I do not see I posit as visible to others; so when I will have walked around to reach this hidden part, I will have joined up with the others behind the object to create a totalization I had already anticipated. And as for the objects behind my back, I sense them coming together to form a world, precisely because they are visible to, and are seen by, others. . . . In short, the others assure the margins and transitions in the world.

Contrary to Sartre's earlier analysis, however, Deleuze argues that this crucial phenomenological significance only comes into view from the effects artificially produced in the novel by the absence of actual others. (In some ways this claim also corresponds to Heidegger's central argument in *Being and Time* concerning the disruption that may occur in the whole structure of the world through the damage or loss of one of its constituent parts.) For example, if we recall the effects caused by the immediate absence of others from Robinson's consciousness in the initial phase of his solitude on the island, they are described as *"optical illusions, mirages, hallucinations, waking dreams, imagined sounds, fantasy and delirium*." These effects occur as a direct result of the absence of an Other-Structure that is normally actualized through the concrete presence of others, causing the relationship between depth, margin, and center in perception-consciousness to fundamentally become disoriented and disorganized.

Second, I have already recounted the gradual transformation of the phenomenological sense attached to Robinson's own body, which becomes merely a neutral object among other objects on the island. In addition, there is also a sense of the violent dispossession of the body's own sexual organization that is the direct result of the absence of others and touches on the struggle between the depths of Robinson's body and the surface that was formerly organized by genital sexuality, specifically the crucial role played by the "good object" that is suddenly discovered to be missing or lost altogether. Many of my fellow castaways will claim that the subject of Robinson in Tournier's version is no different than Defoe's; according to the captain's description, he is also a twenty-two-year-old "typical heterosexual white male" who has abandoned his wife and two children in England. However, this merely assumes that the subject of Robinson at the beginning of Tournier's version is the same Robinson at the end, an assumption that corresponds to many contemporary "theories of the Other" that claim that race or certain organizations of sexuality are substantial components of the Other-Structure, predicated on their phenomenological appearance to consciousness as "thing-like," present-to-hand, and visible to others. Nevertheless, this only proves that the manifestation of race and sexuality can only acquire their *meaning* in the presence of the Other-Structure— for example, when the subjective embodiment of race assumes the same unconscious significance of "origin" that was formerly assigned to the phallus in the organization of sexual difference, and merely represents another phallocentric organization of the body's essential and contingent attributes.

Third, I have already spoken about the gradual fading of Robinson's relationship to his own body as a subjective property (i.e., the phenomenological sense of "having a body that is mine"), but this is also clearly revealed in Robinson's experience of his own nakedness, which undergoes an even more fundamental estrangement. During his self-described periods of "wallowing in the mire," Robinson is defined as the "excrement of Speranza" and often sleeps and defecates without any concern for cleanliness or propriety, which can only exist as a subjective form of concern (or "care," in the Heideggerian sense of *Sorge*). Thus the state of "being naked" is more extreme than the nudity that only addresses the relative relationship of the body's depths and surfaces always from the perspective of the world of others. Rather, Tournier describes the experience of nakedness as a severe exposure to the depths of the body, or as a return to an inorganic substance, as the extreme point of desubjectivation.

> Nakedness is a luxury in which a man may indulge himself without danger only when he is warmly surrounded by his fellow man. For Robinson, while his soul has not yet undergone any change, it was a trial of desperate temerity. Stripped of its threadbare garments—worn, tattered, and sullied, but the fruit of civilized millennia, and impregnated with human associations—his vulnerable body was at the mercy of every hostile element.

Eventually, Robinson's former body is reduced to being an empty surface of pure sensation to every painful blow, every collision, every encounter with objects and other bodies in a flat and desubjectivized space of pure relations. In many ways, this also recalls Emmanuel Levinas's description of a purely impersonal and anonymous plane of Being, of the "there is" (*il y a*) described as the "horror" of a nocturnal space where there is neither object nor even the profile of an object, but rather only a "a swarming of points" that do not refer to one another as in illuminated space, since there is no perspective either. The question we need to ask is what this existential attunement of "horror" that comes from the depths of the body has to do with the surface constituted by sexuality, and what is the relationship of this surface to what Deleuze calls the "Other-Structure"?

Employing the psychoanalytic theories of Freud and Melanie Klein (as well as Lacan's theory of the "symbolic," which is an essential component in Deleuze's own conception of the "Other-Structure"), Deleuze reorients the role played by sexuality in the organization of the relation between the depths of the body produced by the primary processes and the partial surfaces or "territories" produced by the organization of genital sexuality. The construction of the erogenous zones on the body results from the creation of a pure surface that does not have, on its underside, the depth of the body filled with partial objects; rather, the other side of the surface comprises the absence of the lost or missing object that is completely separate from the depths and situated in the field of the Other, according to the well-known Lacanian formulation that "Human desire *is* Other-desire." Recalling Lacan's famous description of the "mirror stage" that precedes the organization of sexuality—and the genital organization, in particular—it is the Ego's jubilant assumption of its own ideal image that becomes the prototype for this separation and subsequent "alienation" (*aphanasis*) of a lost or missing object—namely, the Ego's own *imago,* which can be defined as a pure surface upon which the sexual determination of the "good object" will come to be reflected at a later stage.

Following Klein's insistence on the positive and "reparative" role of the formation of the surfaces produced by the organization of genital sexuality, Deleuze also highlights the function of the phallus defined as the image of the good object projected on the genital zone of the "body without organs" as "restorative" of a surface that mends and protects the Ego itself from the destructive drives that are constantly and violently pushed back into the depths of the body. (In short, the body without organs is literally stitched up so that the body's orifices are closed by the erogenous zones to prevent the depths of the body from leaking out.) "Above all," Deleuze writes, "it is here that the child pursues on his own body the constitution of a surface and the integration of the erogenous zones, thanks to the well-founded privilege of the genital zone"—something, I would add, that occurs repeatedly throughout the subject's sexual

life, especially when the object is repeatedly discovered to be missing, stolen away, or lost altogether. Therefore, it is only from the
"depressive position" that results from the loss of the good object
and the surface that was formerly constituted by genital sexuality
that Deleuze will deduce the crucial role that sexuality plays in
constructing his own theory of the "Other-Structure."

At this point, recalling Tournier's account of Robinson's own
depression after the discovery of the lost or missing object of sexual
desire, the first effect of the absence of the Other-Structure is the
return of the depths constituted by the oral and the anal drives and
the alimentary and excremental partial objects that are introjected into the Ego's own body, but also and more crucially, into the
bodies of others where they will function as the Ego's own partial
objects. Deleuze will interpret this first moment as a regression to
what Klein called the paranoid-schizoid position and the return
of the fragmented body composed of partial objects of the drives.
It is here we discover the real "horror" of the drives, including the
paranoid feelings of being persecuted by the bad introjected objects
of the depths and hallucinatory visions that rise to the surface of
consciousness in dreams. These are the manifestations of the partial objects that are *either* introjected and restrained in the depths
of the body by the organization of genital sexuality *or* projected
into the bodies of others, where they are aggressively pursued and
persecuted—*especially in the body of the mother, which becomes the
prototype for the paranoid-schizoid aggressiveness that the Ego will
project onto all future sexual relations.*

For example, we might recall that in Defoe's original version,
Crusoe is initially overcome by anxiety and the paranoid fear of
being eaten by predators or cannibals, which represents the return
of the paranoid-schizoid aggressiveness of the infantile oral drive.
In Tournier's version, however, recalling the captain's astute diag-
nosis of Robinson's anal-erotic character, we see that the effects of
the return of the anal drive results in Robinson's body being turned
into excrement. *"He relieved himself where he lay, and rarely failed
to roll in the damp warmth of his own excrement. He moved less and*

*less, and his brief excursions always ended in his return to the depths
of the mire. . . . Only his eyes, nose, and mouth were active, alert for
edible weed and toad spawning drifting on the surface."* As an aside,
the role played by the drives and their partial objects might provide
an alternative ontological account of the origin of what Heidegger
called "moods," and particularly anxiousness *(Sichängsten).* Of
course, Heidegger himself would never accept the "ontic" theory
of the primordial role of the drives in infantile consciousness as
even a partial explanation of what he calls the "pre-ontological"
character of existential moods.

Returning to the second phase of Robinson's depressive position,
this is represented by all his attempts to recover the missing or lost
object by projecting it onto the surface of the island that has now
replaced Robinson's own Ego. Accordingly, this phase represents
the depressive position proper that succeeds the manic-schizoid
position of the drives and their partial and introjected objects and,
which again, represented Robinson's attempt to "repair" the surface
that was lost in the previous schizoid stage and was caused by the
initial "disorganization" of genital sexuality. For example, in the
pages of the books that had been erased by the tides and bleached
by the sun, Robinson begins to create a new organization for the
surface of Speranza, constructing articles of government, polity,
penal systems, calendars, days of fasting and celebration, ritual
forms of internment, burial, and commemoration. The fact that all
this work of restoration of the surface appears to take place from
a "a great height," as if from a bird's-eye view of the island itself,
is significant in showing the new distance from the depths of the
body that are affected by the superficial order that Robinson now
constructs on the surface of the island itself. As Deleuze writes:
"Height, in fact, has a strange power of reaction to the depths. It
seems, from the point of height, that depth turns, orients itself in
a new manner, and spreads itself; from a bird's eye view, it is but a
fold easily undone, or rather a local orifice surrounded or stitched to
the surface." Nevertheless, the organization of surfaces constructed
from the depressive position usually succumb to failure in the end,

causing the Ego to crash back into the infinite depths of the body—
that is, its continued vulnerability to all manners of "wallowing in
the mire."

At this point in his interpretation of the fable, however, Deleuze
departs from both Freud and Klein by arguing that a more profound
"splitting" (*Spaltung*) of the subject transcends the division between
the depths of the body constituted by the drives and their partial
objects and the partial surfaces of the erogenous zones constituted by the sexual objects (including any number of the arrangements of genital sexuality that are produced by the perversions).
In fact, the real struggle detected in the reaction of the depressive
position is between the depths of a body containing the explosive,
noxious, and threatening introjected and projected internal objects and what Deleuze calls a "body without organs and without
mechanisms renouncing both projection and introjection" that is
produced primarily as a means of protecting the Ego from its own
body composed of both organs *and* partial objects. This will lead
him to the discovery of a third position, which Deleuze calls "the
sexual-perverse," and can be defined by the autonomy proper to the
organization of its own surfaces and erogenous zones in the relative
absence or negation of the "Other-Structure." In other words, it is
the relative autonomy of the organization of surfaces composed of
erogenous zones that already prefigures the possible separation of
the Ego itself as the "body without organs," which is now opposed
to the bodies produced by the depths of the schizoid position and
the partial surfaces constructed by the depressive position: a body
that takes the Ego itself for the "good object" and, more importantly
for our purposes, substitutes for the original organization of genital sexuality an *anorganic form of immanent desire that no longer
requires the detour through another body.*

It is around the "goal" represented by this third position that
we can now return Deleuze's question of "becoming" that psychoanalysis has only understood negatively as the symptomatic role of
the perversions in resisting the normative function of the Other-
Structure. Following the orientation of Klein, Deleuze assigns per-

version a more positive and potentially transformative role: rather than repairing or reconstructing the broken or damaged surfaces of the body constructed by the erogenous zones, the sexual-perverse position attempts to bypass the origin of sexuality difference altogether and to replace this origin with another goal—that of becoming *"otherwise than the other sex!"* If we examine the "becoming" of Friday-Robinson represented by the third metamorphosis, the first things we should notice is that Robinson has managed to bypass not only the paranoid-schizoid position of the drives that had dominated in the first stage, but also the manic-depressive position in the second stage, since this was too dependent on the subjugation of an external body (first, the body of woman, and then the body of Speranza herself, the earth). As Robinson claims: *"The truth is that given the height to which we have soared, Friday and I, the difference between the sexes has been surpassed."* At this point in the fable, the formerly separated bodies of Robinson and Friday spinning in a white disc until the yoke of Robinson's former body is blended with Friday's yoke, and the single body of Robinson-Friday exhibits *"the beauty of glass and metal and of shining surfaces, a glitter that does not belong to living things."* Finally, once the goal of Robinson-Friday's becoming is achieved, all the sadness and loss that originally belonged to sexuality is now completely surpassed by what Deleuze now calls (for the first time, I believe) a complete "body without organs." *"Voila!"* Deleuze writes, "this is Robinson's final discovery: discovery of the pure surface, of an elemental beyond, of an 'otherwise than another'" (*l'autre qu'autrui*).

This represents the radical Nietzscheanism of Deleuze's moral question concerning the "fantastic principle" of perversion, which was intended to release the surface produced by phantasy from its secondary and derivative position in the organization of "desiring economy" (i.e., Oedipus). It is this positive discovery of a complete body with organs composed of pure elements and surfaces that explains why Deleuze, even in his earlier commentary on the subject of masochism, often claims a positive and transformative role for phantasy as the "virtual" production of desire that expresses a substance of becoming rather than original organic determination of substance by the instincts, as in Freud. Nevertheless, this expression of "becoming" is normally demoted to servicing the imaginary, where the productive and potentially transformative nature of desire is always trapped by the different genital organizations of sexuality that must always refer to the "Other-Structure" for their actualization. In other words, the plane constituted by desire must also detour through the framework of institutions and myths for the most common fantasies that populate the "Other-Structure"— as in the case of the myth of Oedipus and certainly in the case of the fable of Robinson Crusoe! Consequently, the sexual-perverse position risks producing yet another post-Oedipal myth of the same conflict between the depressive and schizoid poles that serves to organize the drives and their partial objects, which is why Deleuze also observes that the body without organs it produces often appears as a "sterile double" of the "Other-Structure."

Finally, at the conclusion of his own research on the question of whether perversion can offer us the "fantastic principle" that will convert sexual difference as an origin into the goal of becoming "otherwise than the other sex," Deleuze must now also acknowledge that the price one must pay for the liberation of a pure and elemental desire is the murder of both the "Other" and of all "the others." Thus the goal of *all perversion is an 'Other-cide' and an 'altruicide.'* Moreover, when the "Other-Structure" is found to be completely absent or somehow negated by purely artificial means, henceforth the only role that "real 'others' can play, in the second structure, is the role of bodies-victims, bodies-doubles, or the role of accomplice-doubles, or the role of accomplices-elements." For example, recalling the third metamorphosis of the fable, it would no longer be even accurate to say that Robinson and Friday can become others to each other since the whole "Other-Structure" is now gone, and along with it, the possibility of another and of all the others! What has taken their place are pure simulacra— that is, pure doubles or twins created to serve a new plane of immanence that assumed the ultimate goal of Robinson's image of

"Great Health," the plane of immanent desire that is produced by a return to primary narcissism.

However, even more troubling are what I have already alluded to earlier as other existential attunements that can be associated with a situation of extreme solitude, attunements of desire that demand nothing less than the sacrifice of the organic body itself as the price one must ultimately pay for producing a complete body without organs. This is true for the body without organs that is produced by alcoholism, certain drug addictions, and naturally, suicide—*and it is certainly true in most of cases involving the body without organs produced by real psychosis and real schizophrenia!* Finally, because he must acknowledge that these dangers also define a process of "becoming" that replaces *an origin* with *a goal,* Deleuze must also conclude that certain *becomings* cannot exist in a world of others, since the world created in the absence of others is composed of an atmosphere that expresses "a strange Spinozism lacking any oxygen in favor of the elemental energy of the drives." For example, concerning the goal that is represented by the final "becoming" of "Robinson-Friday," one can only say: *"They" is longer from this world; "They" now come from the giant sideway ice-planet, Uranus; "They" is now Uranian!*

In conclusion, I began my own investigation by asking what use we might have for yet another fable of Robinson Crusoe today. I have argued that the fable is still useful as a cautionary tale concerning the dangers of living in a world without others, especially since everybody (tout le monde), in a certain respect, lives on a desert island today. However, I also observed, concerning the original fable of Crusoe, that one cannot choose to become a castaway and to live alone on one's own desert island in a world with others, since the "Other-Structure" is the a priori condition of any subject whatsoever. In saying this, I realize—even before the time of the pandemic—that many of my fellow castaways have been experimenting with their own "desert island sexuality" in an attempt to escape the more oppressive and sad effects of the "Other-Structure." I would suggest that the success or failure of your experimentation can be assessed by a simple empirical test that consists of two questions: First question: "How stable is your own body without organs?" Is it relative smooth and seamless, or is it prone to frequent ruptures, causing you to crash back into the depths of the organic body? In other words, is it smooth and round like a hard-boiled egg, flat like a crepe, or does it always come out looking like scrambled eggs? Second question: "What role do you assign the 'others' in your immanent plan of desire?" In other words, are there any real "others" living on your desert island, or only the simulacra of others (e.g., victims, accomplices, co-conspirators, body doubles, and body-organs)?

Sixth Day: The Worst-Case Scenario Lullaby (Bonaparte)

December 8, 2020

Everything I have recounted thus far is only a theoretical description of the real effects made possible by the schizoid and depressive poles, which can only be further exacerbated by the real situation of solitude caused by living on a desert island, as in the case of the purely fictional portrait of Robinson Crusoe. Therefore, at this point I will now depart from the theoretical "instrument of research" deployed by Deleuze's commentary and instead make a few observations from my own phenomenological investigation of living on a desert island these past six months. As I already reported to the reader: I am alone, having neither a Friday, a Tuesday, nor even a companion animal. And yet I am not complaining, since I have also discovered many advantages in my solitude, even convincing myself to welcome my "bachelor" state as a necessary part of my existential research for these reflections, especially when I came to understand that I was never more alone than when I was with others.

However, I must also confess to my reader that I have been haunted by the image of Robinson's decomposing face during the long nights of insomnia, accompanying by the fading vision of the others like lamps in windows on far-distant islands that are being turned off, one by one. On some nights while I lay there gazing at the ceiling above my bed and thought I could see the shadow of Friday circling

above me like a shark. At these moments I began to wonder if I
was already dead, or worse, that given the current situation of the
lockdown, I became persecuted by the idea that, if I died tonight,
the police wouldn't discover my bloated corpse for weeks. The
image of my rotting body became an "idee fixé" of sorts, which kept
me awake and vigilant for many nights, when I would stare at the
dark ceiling for hours hearing in my head the final refrain from the
"Melody X" by the artist Bonaparte: *Something's gotta change . . .
Hold on to something good."*

In the last reflections, I briefly touched on the effects of depression and secondary narcissism caused by solitude, so today I wish
to cover the effects of memory and dreams. As Deleuze says in
the eighteenth series of *Logique du sens* ("On Sexuality"), "We are
schizophrenic while sleeping, but manic-depressive when nearing
the point of awakening." Perhaps the depressive position can be
best represented, however, as the point of awakening in which the
subject never completely awakens; thereby introducing a duration
that can last for days, weeks, months, or even years. In this regard,
it can be compared to the night of pure insomnia. During my own
nightly bouts of insomnia, for example, I began to notice a pattern
in that most memories were negative. The faces of lost or missing
relationships, broken engagements, ex-wives and lovers, betrayed
friendships, and alienated family members and children crowded
my consciousness in the night until I succumbed to exhaustion and
fell unconscious. I was disturbed by this at first, and the residues
of negative memories would linger throughout the days, provok-
ing long periods of depression and what Robinson referred to as
"wallowing in the mire."

Eventually, however, I began to understand the positive role of
memory, including traumatic or negative memories, which can be
explained in reference to the earlier meditations on Heidegger. First
of all, the role of memory can be explained by the withdrawal of the
"Other-Structure" as I described in last week's meditation, which
can also be described in Heidegger's terms as the "world structure"
composed of signs and references to others who are ready-to-hand.

As the "whole structure in all of its constituent" parts gradually withdrew into the past and is no longer actual, the role of memory rises to the surface and becomes more visible and "present-to-hand." This became especially visible during the nights of insomnia, as I have already recounted. The part played by negative and traumatic memories (including memories of physical shocks, accidents, violent incidents, social embarrassment, shameful experiences, moments of personal insult, etc.) can be easily seen as the manifestation of past events when the "referrals" and "references" to people and things in the world were disrupted or broken, and the relations that these references once designated have now been "lit up" by the memory-work. In other words, along with the darkening or withdrawal of the actual world, memory fills in to reconstruct the "whole structure in each of its constituent parts" and thus often chooses negative and traumatic memories to convert them into new "signs" (*Zeichen*) that point to the missing references, as if in an attempt to reconnect them to the "whole structure" of referrals that can relocate Dasein in relation to the world. In some respects, this only serves to further confirm Heidegger's claim that Dasein cannot not "return to the world wherein it was"—however, with the caveat that this world may no longer be present. Consequently, the role of negative memory can now be understood as "reparative," in some respects also related to the discussion of the reparative role of the depressive position in reconstructing the surface of the lost or missing object (the Ego). In this case, during the night of insomnia when consciousness feels itself slipping into nothingness and in the grips of an eternal present and no future except for unconscious sleep, bad or negative memories function exactly like "navigational beacons" (recalling the line I quoted earlier from the poem by Celan) that appear to "light up" the portions of the world that have been covered by darkness. Thus the role of negative memory in particular appears like the night-light in Bonaparte's melody.

But we must ask why negative or traumatic memories are selected, rather than happier or more pleasant memories of Dasein's past. Immediately, however, we would need to ask a following question:

"Selected or chosen by whom?" It is certainly not the subject of Dasein itself that chooses which memories appear to surface in the face of insomnia, since negative memory happens in consciousness like an obsession in which the subject cannot choose, or does not choose, to participate. On one level, it has to do with the intensity of the disruption that first attached itself to the broken or missing reference, which first caused the being or object to be converted and become "present-to-hand" as a "sign" (Zeichen). Thus the work of memory can now repurpose the inventory of signs first created by negative or traumatic events to provide them with new meaning, in the sense of orienting Dasein toward the world to which they belonged, but now with the intensity of obsession and compulsive thinking that often characterizes the manner in which negative memories appear in consciousness in insomnia. On another level, the importance of negative memory returns to Heidegger's axiomatic definition of Dasein as an entity that is in each case "mine" (je meines), and we can see that the character of "mineness" (Jemeinigkeit) is what determines Dasein's relation to negative memory in a manner that is different from happier memories I may have shared with others. For example, the death of a family member, the broken engagement, or the traumatic experience touch Dasein's own being at its core in a manner such that Dasein appears before these experiences and feels in these experiences something that remains unsharable and inexpressible to others. Thus Dasein finds itself "alone" with or alongside its own existence, an experience of ecstasy (ékstasis). At the same time, as I have already argued, this experience of aloneness is somewhat contradictory and even impossible, since Dasein can never be absolutely alone unless there is also the possibility of the others, which is to say, there is no place in the world that Dasein can go to be alone without bringing along all the others, including on a desert island. In other words, desert islands and castaways can only exist in a world with others, even if these others happen to be absent or missing in the place wherein Dasein finds itself. In this case, Dasein must carry along its own others—if only to be able to exist all by itself!—and this will account for the role of negative memory in those situations, like the night of pure insomnia, where Dasein feels that is most alone. At that moment, all the others return, including those beings Dasein either thought it had lost forever or had thought it had sent away and condemned in eternal hatred to exist in pure impersonal Being. Of course, like in Virgil, the damned are often the first ones to return, and they often wear the faces long-lost friends, missing lovers, and also the most hated enemies.

I have also discovered that dreams, particularly what the medical sciences today refer to as "vivid dreams," have a similar "repara-tive" role. If Freud first described defined the dream-work as a combination of the residues from the previous day's experiences, mixed with repressed and unconsciousness memory, in the situation of extreme solitude, vivid dreams can be understood as the residues that belonged to the previous world that are combined with an intensity that might resemble the hallucinatory visions of schizophrenic delirium, following Deleuze's comparison. In this regard, dreaming actually might be understood as a resistance to the depressive position that primarily determines the Ego's con-scious thought during the day, since the primary role of dreams is to construct surfaces and territories on the body without organs. For example, after many nights I began to notice vague patterns in the dream-work that exactly resembled the many-colored fields under the wing of an airplane flying at thirty thousand feet, and these patterns seemed to connect to other fields and territories that disappeared on the horizon, as if the dream-work was recon-structing the entire surface of the world from one zone to the next, field by field, territory by territory (even though "reconstructing" would not be the right word here, since the entire surface of the world does not preexist the production of the partial territories or fields). Upon waking, moreover, I realized that I was always dreaming from a position of great "height," as if the dream-work was fabricating a perfectly smooth surface by flattening out the depths of the body that threatened to engulf my consciousness during the periods of insomnia. It was with this realization that I recalled again

the picture of Celan's later poems, which I had earlier described as
constellations of stars on a black and moonless sky, but which might
also be described as patches of territories constructed on a surface
that is shaped like an orb, or rather, as a conglomeration of images
that look like fields on a series of partial surfaces. St. John of the
Cross described them as "crystal morsels" of dark contemplation
that God sends to some individuals, especially to those like me "who
are not destined to so lofty a degree of love as others." If Deleuze
compared dreams to the schizoid process of investing libidinal energy in the production of surfaces from the erogenous zones and
connecting these zones to the body without organs, we might also
understand the function of dreams as the dynamic formation of a
surface space around a singular zone of the body (the eye, the ear,
the mouth, the lips, the vagina, the anus, etc.) in order to reinvest
the drives in new surfaces produced by the dream images. In fact,
I find an exact correspondence with Celan's habit of constituting
clusters of word images around particular orifices that serve as
"singular points" of the erogenous zones on the body—but once
again, *usually from a perspective or point of view of a great height
that separates the surfaces from the fathomless depths of the body.*

Finally, the third class of images I have already addressed in
the previous meditation around the status of the lost or missing
object—that is, the representatives of "the good object" that still
exists somewhere in the world, having already escaped the island
precisely by having been lost already. Phenomenologically speaking, the exact manner of their apparition in the night of insomnia is akin to hallucination, since the representatives of the lost or
missing object exists in the duration of an eternal present that is
constructed as a "zone" on the body without organs, and which is
usually operated by the Other-Structure through the establishment
of genital sexuality. Here I recall from memory Lacan's little fable
of the lamella from Seminar XI, *The Four Fundamental Concepts of
Psychoanalysis,* the "good object" represents nothing less than the
indestructible, immortal life of the libido! In other words, it em-
bodies that part of the Ego's own primary narcissism that the sexed

being necessarily loses in passing through sexual division (Lacan even compares the unsexed body without organs to an amoeba because it is extra flat and moves around like an amoeba.) If we excuse the humor in Lacan's little fable, it can be seen as the best explanation of how the body without organs survives any division installed by the sexual organization and, moreover, bears no relation to the death or mortality of the sexed living being. It is for this reason, as Lacan says, it can fly off and run around; it can lose to a "good object" only to discover it again elsewhere; moreover, for the purposes of our investigation, because it represents the libido's pure indestructible instinct for life, it can exist in the world even when "the world is gone." In other words, because it is indestructible, it still exists somewhere in the world, whether it lands on the face of a lost lover who is either dead or still living on a desert island somewhere, the face of someone I have never met, or who has just passed me in the next car; perhaps, the iridescent eye of the Moon, the luminous and acephalic body of a distant planet like Saturn, Venus, or Uranus; and, finally, under certain special conditions, the face of God. In fact, the only way you know that it is missing again is when the object that provided it with a temporary surface or facade no longer stares back at you; although, it also has the strange habit of suddenly disappearing one day only to return and land back on the same object the next. This is why I have also insisted on the status of the image of the "good object" as a hallucination, rather than as a memory image, or even a dream image, because the image of the good object is what still relates the Ego to its own indestructible life (i.e., primary narcissism) reflected on a surface that shines brightly with the beauty of metal or glass, the image of a gaze that is *possessed* by the Ego as the missing piece of its own pure and indestructible desire. Nevertheless, in this image there is still present a fundamental dehiscence between the anonymous and essentially impersonal nature of desire and the living being who constitutes its most outward and superficial *apparition,* since it was only by chance to begin with that the Ego happened to suddenly rediscover its own image in another person who appears on the body without organs like Venus rising from the waves. Finally, it is interesting that Lacan also concludes his little fable with a warning that the missing lamella could also return some night and envelope your face while you are sleeping and suffocate you, since a body without organs, according to Antonin Artaud's original formula, has "no mouth, no teeth, no larynx." This basically reasserts the same caution I expressed toward the body without organs that can be produced by the return of primary narcissism, and why earlier I chose to interpret the final metamorphosis in Tournier's version of Robinson's "solar sexuality" as either a pure schizoid phantasy or the hallucinatory deliria of real schizophrenia or real psychosis. Therefore, in conclusion, to add a note of caution to my fellow castaways, I will recall again the lyric of Bonaparte's dark melody that has become my own personal talisman to stand guard against the possibility of the lamella's return while I am sleeping: "Hold on to something good"; at the same time: *keep it at a safe distance!* But, above all: *"keep the night-light on!"*

Seventh Day: Robinson? C'est Moi!

December 29, 2020

> It is as reasonable to represent one kind of imprisonment by
> another, as it is to represent anything that really exists by that
> which exists not.
>
> —DANIEL DEFOE

This morning I found a bottle that had washed up on the beach.
I actually don't know if it had come in on the tide last night, or if
it has been there days and perhaps even weeks. This is because
I stopped going down to the beach several weeks ago, because
the sight of the dead that were piled up like driftwood became too
distressing, and the new corpses came each night—over eighty
thousand since I last counted in June—and the smell was becoming unbearable until the birds picked all the flesh from their
bones and what remained of the bodies was finally desiccated
by the sun. As the reader might have already guessed, the bottle I found contained a small note written on the single leaf of
bleached paper. It read: "HOLD ON. OTHERS ARE COMING. YOU
ARE SAVED!" At first I thought this was a practical joke by some
other castaway, and I imagined him stuffing the same message
in an empty bourbon bottle, which he had drained the night before, and tossing it into the sea thinking at least the message
would bring some hope to another wretch like him, even if this
hope ultimately turned out to be false. I hope this is not the case,
and so I tried to hold on to an attitude of cautious optimism that
the message was indeed genuine and that the "others were coming." Immediately, I began to trace the horizon to see if I could
catch the flash of a plane's silver fuselage or the liquid trail of

aviation fuel at forty thousand feet. But there was nothing but
empty sky with gulls that were chattering like tourists around a
monument of bloated corpses.

This will be my final entry since I have set my eyes on the horizon
most of these past days and toward a possible world to come. Still,
as of this date in late December, exactly six months since I began
these reflections, the pandemic is still not over, and not even the
ending is in sight. Help may be on the way, according to the message
in the bottle, but it has not yet arrived, and not another soul has
stepped foot on the beach of my desert island and raised their arms
with the promise of a lasting and tearful embrace. Nevertheless, I
will not waste any time left on the island by dipping my feet into
the shallow waters of platitude concerning "lessons learned." My
only purpose was to record some of the more deleterious effects
of my own solitude and to give some words of hope (and caution)
for the benefit of fellow castaways who have been locked down on
their own desert islands. Even though I stated at the beginning of
this fictional monologue of a castaway on a desert island that I was
pretending to speak for everybody (tout le monde), I am also very
well aware that I have not speaking for "everyone." There are still
"others" who have either chosen to remain or have been stranded
on the mainland—so-called first responders, including doctors,
nurses, bus drivers, and grocery clerks. Of course, as in the case
of every plague in history, the poorest classes have been left behind by those who have the means of escaping to their own islands.
However, I have never held any pretense of "speaking for them"
like so many liberal journalists and intellectuals have done over the
past six months from the relative safety of their own desert islands.
(The very act of speaking *to all the others for the others* is the kind
of hypocritical doublespeak that intellectuals are historically guilty
for engaging in, even when we were not in a pandemic or plague.)
Besides, during the periods of the lockdowns, even bus drivers and
grocery clerks were forced to return each night to their own islands,
even though this resulted in the spread of the contagion to members of their families and loved ones, and so I hope that some part

of my monologue can still speak *to them,* if not *for them,* as well. So instead of standing on the beach searching the horizon for the first signs of Celan's airplane, this morning I went back into the part of my retreat where I have stored my library on a stone shelf where the dampness didn't get to it, and I found my sun-bleached copy of Camus's *La Peste.* I thought it might be a better use of my time reading the ending to discover any "lessons learned" from the last plague, especially since the difference between the plague recounted by Camus's narrator and our own is only a change of one consonant—that is, bats instead of rats.

As the reader may recall, the novel recounts the events of a fictional plague that occurs in the town of Oran on the northern Algerian coast in the year "194X." The narrator is later revealed to be Dr. Bernard Rieux, a physician and "first responder," who chronicles the events of the plague that begins on April 16 and lasts for almost a full year, officially ending on January 25. Before the lockdown began, I was still teaching an undergraduate course at the university on "existentialism," and Camus's later novels *L'Etranger* and *La Chute* were on the syllabus for the spring semester, but I decided not to teach *La Peste* because of its length and also because I didn't believe that the novel would speak as resonantly to a group of twenty-year-old undergraduates. Therefore, it was a bit of an irony when reports of the Covid-19 virus that supposedly was spreading from Wuhan, China, began circulating in the media beginning around the end of January 2020, and then gained in volume and proximity to the campus until the shutdown of the university occurred on March 16—one month before the fictional date of the beginning of the plague in the novel—and I was forced to teach online from my new desert island post in Fayetteville, a small village on the Finger Lakes outside Syracuse, New York.

It was then that I threw the rest of the course syllabus out and assigned the novel to the students—most of whom were now secluded at home with their families, or locked down in small apartments around Syracuse, especially the international students who couldn't travel home by mid-March—asking them to read one part each week and keep a personal diary of their own experiences of the time of plague that they were now also living through. We immediately discovered an "uncanny" verisimilitude between Dr. Rieux's account of the pattern of events that took place in the city of Oran that fateful spring and the events that were unfolding daily through media reports and through our own experiences of the reactions on the part of our own "townspeople." This included the initial state of denial concerning the reality of the plague, which was most prominently vocalized by politicians, but also realized through the reactions of reckless and wanton behavior on the part of the people themselves. However, this was soon followed by expressions of panic and fear as the reality of the pandemic finally sunk in among most, which occurred about a month later (mid-May in the novel and around mid-April in real life) when the tangible evidence of the plague could be quantified in the number of corpses it produced each day, or in the media footage of corpses piled on top of one another in the makeshift morgues in hospital gift shops, in long rows of refrigerated trucks that lined the streets around the hospitals in New York city, and, finally, in pictures of soccer stadiums converted into either ICU wards or morgues in European cities like Madrid, Barcelona, Venice, and Milan.

This synchronicity continued throughout each chapter of the novel, corresponding to each week of the pandemic between the months of March and early May, and I can only recommend that readers put this novel on their own desert island reading list or, if they didn't think to pack it before the shipwreck, that they take some time if and when they return home to read it. I could go on recounting the details of Camus's somewhat prophetic description of our own time of plague, but instead will simply quote an observation made by Rieux that appears as a long internal monologue in the first chapter, since I believe its relevance will be more than apparent to the contemporary reader and fellow castaway:

> A pestilence isn't a thing made to man's measure; therefore we tell ourselves that pestilence is a mere bogy of the mind, a bad dream that will pass away. But it doesn't always pass away and, from one

bad dream to another, it is men who pass away, and the humanists first of all, because they haven't taken their precautions. Our townsfolk were not more to blame than others; they forgot to be modest, that was all, and thought that everything still was possible for them; which presupposed that pestilences were impossible. They went on doing business, arranged for journeys, and formed views. How should they have given a thought to anything like plague, which rules out any future, cancels journeys, silences the exchange of views. They fancied themselves free, and no one will ever be free so long as there are pestilences.

It is from this passage we might understand the significance of the epilogue from Defoe's own plague diaries, which Camus chose for the novel, and that states as a rule of genre that one kind of imprisonment can be represented by another, just as it is allowable to represent anything that really exists by something that does not. In other words, a plague or a pandemic is also a kind of imprisonment, or existential loss of freedom, just as the kind of imprisonment that a pandemic necessarily entails can also be represented by the fiction of living on a desert island. (At least, this is how I have understood the law of genre that governs Camus's own fictional account of the plague in "194X" and have simply applied it to govern my own fictional account of living on a desert island during the time of the pandemic in 2020).

At this point, however, I will now skip to the conclusion of the novel in part five, which takes place in the month of January. Given the uncanny accuracy of Camus's description of the train of events that took place during the first eight months since the pandemic began, especially when the gates to the city were shut and the townspeople were forced to "shelter in place," one would naturally guess that his account of the last month of the plague, before it suddenly dissipated on or around January 25, will be equally clairvoyant. So I retrieved my copy again and began to mark up passages from a past that seemed like accurate predictions of my future. Soon, however, I realized that I had highlighted so many parts with a piece of charcoal I had drawn from the fire that the pages were now black and almost illegible. Consequently, I have decided to quote two passages from the end of the account that take place the moment when the plague began to retreat from the city and the people began to come out of their isolation, since this is the day that most of us have been dreaming of for the better part of 2020.

Over a relatively brief period the disease lost practically all the gains piled up over many months. Its setbacks with seemingly predestined victims, like Grand and Rieux's girl patient, its bursts of activity for two or three days in some districts synchronizing with its total disappearance from others, its new practice of multiplying its victims on, say, a Monday, and on Wednesday letting almost all escape, in short, its accesses of violence followed by spells of complete inactivity, all these gave an impression that its energy was flagging, out of exhaustion and exasperation, and it was losing, with its self-command, the ruthless, almost mathematical efficiency that had been its trump card hitherto. Of a sudden Castel's anti-plague injections scored frequent successes, denied it until now. Indeed, all the treatments the doctors had tentatively employed, without definite results, now seemed almost uniformly efficacious. It was as if the plague had been hounded down and cornered, and its sudden weakness lent new strength to the blunted weapons so far used against it. Only at rare moments did the disease brace itself and make as it were a blind and fatal leap at three or four patients whose recovery had been expected, a truly ill-starred few, killed off when hope ran highest.

[. . .]

It must, however, be admitted that our fellow citizens' reactions during that month were diverse to the point of incoherence. More precisely, they fluctuated between high optimism and extreme depression. Hence the odd circumstance that several more attempts to escape took place at the very moment when the statistics were most encouraging. This took the authorities by surprise, and, apparently, the sentries too, since most of the "escapists" brought it off. But, looking into it, one saw that people who tried to escape at this time were prompted by quite understandable motives. Some of them the plague had imbued with a skepticism so thorough that it was now a second nature; they had become allergic to hope in any form. Thus, even when the plague had run its course, they went on living by its standards. They were, in short, behind the times. In the case of others, chiefly those who had been living until now in forced separation from those they loved, the rising wind of hope, after all these months of durance and depression, had fanned impatience to a blaze and swept away their self-control. They were seized with a sort of panic at the thought that they might die so near the goal and never see again the ones they loved, and their long privation have no recompense. Thus, though for weary months and months they had endured their long ordeal with dogged perseverance, the first thrill of hope had been enough to shatter what fear and hopelessness had failed to impair. And in the frenzy of their haste, they tried to outstrip the plague, incapable of keeping pace with it up to the end.

Both passages, it seems to me, speak of an exhaustion of sorts. The first passage describes the exhaustion of the virus itself as if it was a marathon runner who finally runs out of the last ounce of energy and collapses on the pavement only a hundred yards from the finish line, or perhaps the exhaustion that occurs when a wildfire that has raged through the countryside and burned over a million acres, including houses and livestock, finally smolders and dies because of the lack of any more fuel. The second sense of exhaustion concerns the hope and perseverance of the townspeople themselves, many of whom exhibit completely opposite reactions ranging from skepticism and denial ("Thus, even when the plague had run its course, they went on living by its standards"), to panic and complete loss of self-control ("And in the frenzy of their haste they tried to outstrip the plague, incapable of keeping pace with it up to the end"). In both senses, Camus seems to record a strange symmetry between the plague and the people, as if they were parts of the same organism and thus expressed the same pattern of behavior because they were one living thing.

The most visible signs of this parallelism can be seen in the sudden outburst of frenetic and desperate activity that occurs in both parts of the organism simultaneously, which can be explained physiologically as a common symptom that happens when an animal is about to die and it suddenly exhibits an increase in expenditure of its last ounce of energy, or its last gasp of breath. For example, I have heard stories from hunters of an elk that had been shot in the heart, which manages to run several more miles even though it was already physiologically dead, or of a plane accident victim who walks away from the crash and gets several miles before finally collapsing, even though the victim was missing half of his head and was already brain-dead. Consequently, in the passages above we seem to witness a similar phenomenon on the part of the plague, which in the end seemed to "brace itself and make as it were a blind and fatal leap at three or four patients whose recovery had been expected," and the townspeople, for whom "the rising wind of hope, after all these months of durance and depression, had fanned impatience to a blaze and swept away their self-control."

At this point, I will longer maintain the fiction of my desert island genre, and so I will refer to contemporary events to further illustrate this strange parallelism, or rather, this underlying symmetry between the behavior of the virus and human behavior that seems to imply that they are both parts of the same giant organism. For example, in the last weeks of December 2020, it seemed that the virus was finally defeated, with the approval of the vaccines for Covid-19, and the politicians and the media were uniformly declaring we were now close to the end of the pandemic. However, almost on exactly the same day that vaccines were beginning to be administered in the UK, there was the sudden discovery of a new variant that appeared exactly as if the virus was indeed bracing itself and making a desperate leap at the human populations again, immediately prompting a new and more severe round of lock-down orders across the European continent and the banning of passengers on flights from the UK to almost every airport around the world. In other words, just at the moment when the gates to the city of Oran were opened, they were quickly slammed shut again and the townspeople were again prisoners of the same pestilence. If this synchronicity of events is not already compelling enough, one only has to consider the fact that the date of the appearance of the new variant of Covid-19, which is now raging around the globe, occurs almost exactly one year from the first visible appearance of the virus in Wuhan, Verona, and Seattle toward the end of December 2019.

Concerning similar signs of "impatience" that have occurred almost simultaneously in the human part of the organism, I will quote from an email (i.e., "message in a bottle") I received this morning from a former student in Seoul, Korea. After wishing me a "Happy 2021," the student reports: "Although I can't compare it to the U.K., South Korea is also really serious. The number of confirmed covid-19 cases has exceeded 1,000 per day. Many people are still going out for their own enjoyment. It's tragic." At the same time, there has been a rise in the number of what Camus calls "escapists" in the United States, where there has been a remarked increase in signs of impatience and loss of self-control on the part of populations, often culminating in "blind and deadly leaps," including large gatherings where people refuse to wear masks, and well over one million travelers in airports across the country, even while the number of cases and confirmed deaths continue to blaze and rise higher each day with no ending in sight.

What do we make of this uncanny parallelism, or this strange symmetry of the same pattern of behavior expressed by the virus and the townspeople? At the risk of anthropomorphizing the virus—that is, by applying the motives that are offered to explain the behavior of the human side of the organism to deduce the possible motives for the behavior of the virus—can we impute this "blind and fatal leap" of the virus to something like "exacerbation," "panic," "the first thrill of hope," "frenzy," "rage," or "desperate bid for freedom"? As I was meditating on this question, I recalled a passage from the last chapter of Whitehead's *Process and Reality*—a book I didn't think to bring with me, and so I don't even need to maintain the fiction of my desert island library in this case—where he defines the essential characteristic of life as a kind of desperate "bid for more freedom." If I recall the passage correctly, Whitehead ascribes to nature something like a motive that appears behind every act of theft or robbery, in which life steals through the environment comprising both organic and inorganic societies in order to find "an empty space in a desperate bid for freedom," which he further defines as an intense "craving for satisfaction." For example, is this comparable to the empty space that the virus initially found in the living cells of bats, which then, in pursuing its own satisfaction, led the virus on a chain of robberies through the empty spaces it then discovered in the respiratory system of the human populations? To recall Deleuze's question from the previous meditation concerning whether or not sexuality can offer us the fantastic principle that replaces an "origin" with a "goal" (i.e., becoming), in his definition of nature I believe that Whitehead already offers us an even more fantastic principle, which is the principle of life itself, since life has no "origin" and knows only *becomings*. In fact, the principle also recalls Heidegger's earlier definition of life is "a domain of openness which possesses as wealth [i.e., becoming] with which the human world [and human sexuality in particular] may have nothing to compare."

To this image of viral life we must now pose another image that appears in Camus's description of the completely opposite reaction on the part of the townspeople: "Some of them the plague had imbued with a skepticism so thorough that it was now a second nature; they had become allergic to hope in any form. Thus, even when the plague had run its course, *they went on living by its standards.*" What would it mean to continue to live by the standards established by the pandemic? To maintain social distancing, to continue to wear masks even after the last signs of the virus have dissipated in memory? Or, according to the thesis I have been pursuing throughout the course of these meditations, to continue to live in a world without others? In my view, this is the prophetic vision that Camus already offers us at the conclusion of the last plague, and which I will adapt to describe our own post-Covid world: a world in which roughly half the human population continues to live on a desert island (although, certainly, only the half that has the means to afford it), while the other half is forced to live with the deleterious effects of the pandemic and who must risk their life daily in their desperate bid for freedom (i.e., satisfaction, justice, the right to inhabit, etc.).

To conclude today's last reflection, I have often been astonished during the past six months by the admiration extolled to those societies for their "resilience" in defending themselves against the virus—by virtue of the fact that they are also the most closed, ethnocentric, politically totalitarian, and immunologically controlled! If I were now to speculate concerning this new immunological order that will emerge as a principle of sovereignty to govern the global system in the post-Covid environment, I might define this principle according to the following maxim: the most beautiful world is also that which is perfectly closed. Thus it would be a world that has managed to seal off every empty space, and every orifice among its human population, precisely to prevent life from breaking in in its own bid for freedom. (It would be like the moon, or a planet, like Uranus.) First, however, to create the most perfect society, it will be necessary first to change the species. In other words, if the Greeks had established the concept of the previous world, since the time of Aristotle, by defining its primary inhabitants as "political animals" (that is, animals who live in a city and thus whose primary trait is defined as "sociability"), then the concept of the world that is being fashioned by the new immunological order is certainly no longer Greek. In fact, the primary problem with the Greek concept of the world according to an immunological point of view is that it left open too many empty spaces for life to break in. As far as the new world and its inhabitants, therefore, we are no longer even "late-born Greeks," like Heidegger, but rather "posthuman." And perhaps the posthuman will one day be defined by ethnologists as "the most solitary animal" *(animal solitarium),* the animal that will have been discovered to have lived alone on a desert island, who was reported to be heard on some nights calling out to himself from deep inside his cave—*"Robinson?" Followed by the reply—"C'est moi!"*

The Complete Desert Island Library

Camus, Albert. *La Peste*. Paris: Editions Gallimard, 1947.

Camus, Albert. *The Plague, The Fall, The Exile and the Kingdom*. New York: Everyman's Library, 2004.

Celan, Paul. *Collected Prose*. Translated by Rosemary Waldrop. London: Carcanet Press, 1986.

Celan, Paul. *Gesammelte Werke*. 3 vols. Berlin: Surkamp, 1986.

Coetzee, J. M. *Foe*. London: Penguin Books, 1986.

Defoe, Daniel. *Robinson Crusoe*. New York: W. W. Norton, 1994.

Deleuze, Gilles. *Logique du sens*. Paris: Minuit, 1969.

Derrida, Jacques. *The Beast and the Sovereign, vol. 2*. Translated by Geoffrey Bennington. Chicago: University of Chicago Press, 2020.

Heidegger, Martin. *Being and Time*. New York: Harper & Row, 1962.

Heidegger, Martin. *Die Grundbegriffe der Metaphysik: Welt-Endlichkeit-Einsamkeit*. Frankfurt am Main: Kostermann RoteReiche, 2018.

Heidegger, Martin. *Existence and Existents*. Translated by Alphonse Lingis. Pittsburgh, Pa.: Duquesne University Press, 1977.

Heidegger, Martin. *The Fundamental Concepts of Metaphysics*. Translated by William McNeill and Nicolas Walker. Bloomington: Indiana University Press, 1995.

Heidegger, Martin. "Question concerning Technology." In *Basic Writings*, edited by David Farrell Krell, 307–42. London: Harper, 1993.

Heidegger, Martin. *Sein und Zeit*. Tübingen: Max Niemeyer Verlag, 1972.

Levinas, Emmanuel. *De l'existence à l'existant*. Paris: Vrin, 2013.

St. John of the Cross. *The Collected Works of St. John of the Cross*. Translated by Kieran Kavanaugh and Otilio Rodriguiez. Washington, D.C.: ICS, 1973.

Tournier, Michel. *Friday*. Translated by Norman Denny. Baltimore, Md.: Johns Hopkins Press, 1997.

Tournier, Michel. *Vendredi ou les limbes du Pacifique*. Paris: Éditions Gallimard, 1967.

Végsó, Roland. *Worldlessness after Heidegger: Phenomenology, Psychoanalysis, Deconstruction*. Edinburgh: Edinburgh University Press, 2020.

(Continued from page iii)

Forerunners: Ideas First

Gregg Lambert is Dean's Professor of Humanities in the College of Arts and Sciences at Syracuse University. His most recent University of Minnesota Press books include *The Elements of Foucault* (2020) and *Philosophy after Friendship: Deleuze's Conceptual Personae* (2017).